In Science Curiosity

Seiko Otsuka
Hiroki Takikawa
Sachie Kiyokawa

Supervised by
Atsushi Mukuhira

KINSEIDO

Kinseido Publishing Co., Ltd.

3-21 Kanda Jimbo-cho, Chiyoda-ku,
Tokyo 101-0051, Japan

Copyright © 2021 by   Seiko Otsuka
                      Hiroki Takikawa
                      Sachie Kiyokawa
                      Atsushi Mukuhira

First published 2021 by Kinseido Publishing Co., Ltd.

Cover design   Nampoosha Co., Ltd.
Text design   C-leps Co., Ltd.

音声ファイル無料ダウンロード

http://www.kinsei-do.co.jp/download/4123

この教科書で 🎧 DL 00 の表示がある箇所の音声は、上記 URL または QR コードにて
無料でダウンロードできます。自習用音声としてご活用ください。

▶ PC からのダウンロードをお勧めします。スマートフォンなどでダウンロードされる場合は、
　 ダウンロード前に「**解凍アプリ**」を**インストール**してください。
▶ URL は、**検索ボックスではなくアドレスバー（URL 表示欄）**に入力してください。
▶ お使いのネットワーク環境によっては、ダウンロードできない場合があります。

◎ CD 00　左記の表示がある箇所の音声は、教室用 CD（Class Audio CD）に収録されています。

はじめに

　世界は未知の現象にあふれています。

　正確にいえば、現象そのものには慣れ親しんでいるとしても、なぜそのようなことが起こるのか、どのような仕組みになっているのか、うまく説明できない場合がしばしばあります。雨後の空にかかる七色の虹は、なぜアーチ型なのか。直射日光を浴びると、どうして人の体は赤く黒くなっていくのか。地球が太陽の周りをずっと回っているのはなぜか。なかには、ある地域の人々にはごくあたりまえの出来事なのに、別の地域の人々は生涯一度も経験しないこともあります。大人にとっては常識だとしても、幼い子どもには驚きでしかないこともあり、またその逆もありえます。ただ、現代においてその仕組みが明らかにされているあらゆる現象に共通することは、ある人がある時それを不思議に感じ、好奇心を抱き、その仕組みを探求した結果、今私たちはその仕組みを理解できているということです。好奇心は、科学的進展の原動力なのです。

　もう一つ、言えることがあります。さまざまな現象やその仕組みについて多くの人々が知っているということは、つまり、それが説明されたり理解するための言葉が生み出され、共有されている、ということです。現象を説明する言葉が存在しなければ、それは人々の共有知識にはなりえません。言葉の限界は、科学の限界です。逆にいえば、科学的解明が切り開く地平は、言葉が進化する新たな地平でもあります。

　本書 *In Science Curiosity* は、私たちの体から宇宙まで、さまざまなスケールで存在する自然現象について子どもが投げかける好奇な質問に対して、大人である専門家が回答した Web 記事に基づく教材です。専門家の説明は、当然、子どもに理解してもらえるように平易な英語で書かれています。本書を利用する皆さんは、まずは子どもの気持ちで好奇心を燃やしながら、専門家の説明をじっくり正確に理解してみましょう。そして次に、専門家の立場に身を置いて、つまり、自分が誰かに説明するという仮定で、この英文から得られる語彙や構文を最大限に活用して、科学的な英語表現の初歩的運用力を鍛えてみましょう。そうすれば、専門家の説明で明かされる科学的真理の地平が、皆さんの英語運用力の新たな到達点となるはずです。

　本書の作成過程で、金星堂の池田恭子さんにはさまざまな角度からの適切な助言やあり余る激励をいただきました。とても言葉では尽くせませんが、紙面をお借りして感謝申し上げます。

2020年夏

編著者・監修者一同

■ Contents ■

Why Is Air Colder the Higher Up You Go?

▬ Starting Words

1 ～ 6 の語に合う英語と日本語の意味をそれぞれ選び、(　　　) に書き入れましょう。

🎧 DL 002　◎ CD1-02

Words	English Definitions	Japanese Definitions
1. radiation (　　) (　　)	**A** a tiny portion, fragment or amount	**ア** 吸収する
2. altitude (　　) (　　)	**B** to be all around something	**イ** 粒子
3. particle (　　) (　　)	**C** a form of energy that comes especially from nuclear reactions	**ウ** 放射線
4. surround (　　) (　　)	**D** to throw back light, heat, etc. from a surface of something	**エ** 反射する
5. absorb (　　) (　　)	**E** the height of an object above the sea	**オ** 取り囲む
6. reflect (　　) (　　)	**F** to take in substance from the surface around something	**カ** 標高

▬ I Want to Know This!

枠内の問いについて、あなたならどのように答えますか。クラスで話し合いましょう。

Why is air colder the higher up you go? Shouldn't it be hotter as you're getting closer to the Sun?

_____

_____

_____

■ Here's a Key for You

次の英文は、前ページの問いに対する専門家による回答です。

A 音声を聴いて、[　　　]に入る語を書き取りましょう。

B 英文を読んで理解しましょう。

🎧 DL 003 ～ 008　◎ CD1-03 ～ ◎ CD1-08

❶ As you may know, hot air rises. So why is it so cold at the top of a mountain? Well, it helps if you imagine the ground here on Earth as a big heater. It keeps us warm, and if you move away from the heater you feel cold.

❷ So what "heats up" the heater? The light and warmth from the Sun. Scientists call
5　this light and warmth "[**1.**　　　　　　　]".

❸ The light and warmth from the Sun travel through space towards Earth, and pass through our atmosphere. (The "atmosphere" is what we call the swirling air that [**2.**　　　　　　　] our planet.) But the atmosphere isn't very good at holding onto the warmth from the Sun. The heat just slips straight through it. (That's because air
10　at higher [**3.**　　　　　　　] thins out as the gas [**4.**　　　　　　] expand and lose energy.) Eventually, the heat from the Sun hits the ground and the ground soaks it up.

❹ This especially happens in forests and oceans, which are very good at absorbing
15　heat. Other places, like snow fields, are more likely to [**5.**　　　　　] the radiation—meaning it bounces back toward the Sun instead of being soaked up by the ground.

20　❺ The higher up you go, the further you are away from the "heater" that is keeping us all warm—the ground that has [**6.**　　　　　　　] the warmth from the Sun. At the top of mountains, it can get so cold people could die within minutes without special protection. That's because the air up there is just really bad at "holding onto" the radiation coming from the Sun, and the warmth passes straight through it on its journey toward the ground.

5 ❻ And all the way up in space, there is a lot more radiation from the Sun, and astronauts wear special suits to protect themselves from it. But there's also no air in space, which means there's really nothing much at 10 all to "hold onto" the warmth of the Sun and make the temperature around you feel warm. So if you were unlucky enough to get caught in space without a suit, you would freeze to death before the Sun's radiation 15 would get you.

Notes

    atmosphere「大気」 **swirling air**「渦巻き状の空気」 **hold onto ~**「～を蓄えておく」 **slip through ~**「～を滑り抜ける」 **thin out**「薄くなる」 **expand**「膨張する」 **soak up ~**「（日光など）を吸収する」 **bounce back**「跳ね返る」

A 本文の内容に当てはまるものには T、当てはまらないものには F を（　　　）に書き入れましょう。

1. The atmosphere absorbs radiation from the Sun and works as a heater to keep us warm.　　　　　　　　　　　　　　　　　　　　　　　　（　　）

2. A snow field is better at absorbing heat than forests and oceans.　　（　　）

3. Without special protection, we would die at the top of mountains and in space because of the cold.　　　　　　　　　　　　　　　　　　（　　）

B 放射線と熱について表した以下の説明の（　　　）に適切な日本語を書き入れましょう。

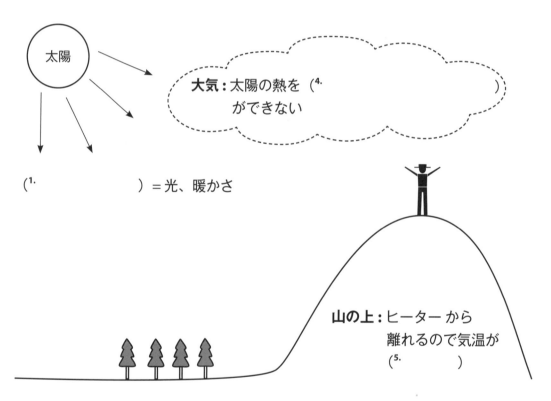

太陽

大気：太陽の熱を（^{4.}　　　　　　　　）
ができない

（^{1.}　　　　　　　）＝光、暖かさ

山の上：ヒーターから
離れるので気温が
（^{5.}　　　　）

地面：
・大きな（^{2.}　　　　　　　）の役割
・森や海は熱を（^{3.}　　　　）しやすい

For Better Understanding

「比較級」の用法を学習しましょう。

2つ以上のものの状態や程度を比べるときには「比較級」を用います。

〈比較級の作り方〉
通常：形容詞・副詞の語尾に〈-er〉をつける
例）warm → warmer　　long → longer
3音節以上などの長い単語：形容詞・副詞の前に〈more〉をつける
例）beautiful → more beautiful　　famous → more famous
不規則変化
例）good, well → better　　bad, ill → worse

また、比較の対象を明確に示す場合には、〈than〉が共に用いられます。

例文 1　The air at the top of mountains is **colder than** that at the foot of mountains.
「山の上の空気はふもとの空気よりも冷たいです」

本文に出てくるように、比較級を用いた次のような表現も覚えておきましょう。
〈the ＋比較級＋主語＋動詞 , the ＋比較級＋主語＋動詞〉「～すればするほど…」

例文 2　**The higher** up you go, **the further** you are away from the "heater" that is keeping us all warm.
「より高い場所に行けば行くほど、私たちみんなを暖かく保っている『ヒーター』から遠ざかることになります」

Grammar for Practice

A　日本語訳を参考に、（　　　）に適切な語を書き入れましょう。

1. This mountain is (　　　　　　　　　) than that mountain.
この山は、あの山よりも高いです。

2. The ground keeps warmth from the Sun (　　　　　　　) than the air.
地面は空気よりも太陽からの暖かさをうまく保持します。

3. (　　　　　) (　　　　　　　　　) you go away from the campfire, (　　　　　)
(　　　　　　) you'll feel.
キャンプファイアから遠くに行けば行くほど、あなたは寒く感じるでしょう。

B 日本語訳に合うように、[   ] 内の語句を並べ替えましょう。

1. 環境に対する放射熱の影響は、科学者たちが予想していたよりも強かったことが明らか
になりました。

The effects of radiation heat in the environment turned out to be _____

_____.

[had / than / expected / the scientists / stronger]

2. 科学者たちは、太陽はその寿命の半分より少し手前にあると予測しており、さらに 65
億年続くと予測しています。

Scientists predict the Sun is _____

through its lifetime and will last another 6.5 billion years.

[less / a / than / little / halfway]

One More Tip プレゼンテーション

このセクションでは、ペアワークを通して英語で発信する力を養います。まずは、
プレゼンテーションの基礎である、自己紹介とトピック・センテンスについて学び
ましょう。
人前で話すときには、発表者はまず名前・所属等の簡単な自己紹介・あいさつを行
います。「何について話すのか」を分かりやすいトピック・センテンスで始めること
も大切です。

■自己紹介
  ・Let me just start by introducing myself.
  ・I am / My name is ... from XX university, Faculty of YY.
■トピック・センテンス
  ・My topic is ....
  ・I will talk about ....

Your Turn

ペアワークのパートナーに、自己紹介を行いましょう。所属のほかにも趣味や興味
のあることなどを取り入れ、相手が興味を持って聴いてくれそうな工夫をしてみま
しょう。

I am _____ from _____, Faculty of
_____. Today, I will talk about _____....

Why Do Leaves Change Color?

Starting Words

1 ～ 6 の語に合う英語と日本語の意味をそれぞれ選び、(　　　) に書き入れましょう。

 DL 009　　CD1-09

Words	English Definitions	Japanese Definitions
1. drop (　　) (　　)	**A** to become hard as a result of extreme cold	**ア** 破壊する
2. destroy (　　) (　　)	**B** to damage something very badly	**イ** 凍る
3. store (　　) (　　)	**C** to allow something to fall	**ウ** 色合い
4. shade (　　) (　　)	**D** relaxed in a pleasant way	**エ** 蓄える
5. freeze (　　) (　　)	**E** a particular form of a color	**オ** 快適な
6. comfortable (　　) (　　)	**F** to put in another place to use later	**カ** 落とす

I Want to Know This!

枠内の問いについて、あなたならどのように答えますか。クラスで話し合いましょう。

There is a nice, big window in my room. On some days at the end of summer, I've found that I can enjoy the colors of the trees through it. Why do leaves change color in autumn?

_____

_____

_____

Here's a Key for You

次の英文は、前ページの問いに対する専門家による回答です。

A 音声を聴いて、[　　　] に入る語を書き取りましょう。

B 英文を読んで理解しましょう。

🎧 DL 010～018　　◎ CD1-10 ～ ◎ CD1-18

❶ In the autumn, lots of plants throw away their leaves. By [**1.**　　　　　　　　　　]
them they are saving their nutrients for the next summer. For plants to grow, they
need sunlight, nutrients, and water. The nutrients and water come from the soil.

❷ To capture sunlight, the leaves use a chemical called chlorophyll, which is what
5　makes leaves green. Chlorophyll turns sunlight into food, through a process called
photosynthesis.

❸ In summer, plants do lots of photosynthesis, because they get lots of light and
because it is warm. The food they make is sugar, which they use to grow new leaves,
flowers, and seeds. In winter, things are less [**2.**　　　　　　　　　　]. The days
10　get shorter, it gets colder and there is less sunshine. When it gets really cold, and
freezes, their leaves can be damaged.

❹ If you want to see what freezing
does to different leaves, take some
different leaves and put them in your
15　freezer. Leave them for a day to get
really cold, then take them out again.
Put them on a plate so you don't make
a mess, then just wait for them to warm
up (this will take a while).

20　**❺** For plants with leaves that don't like to be [**3.**　　　　　　　　　　], winter is a bad
time. Their leaves are all going to be [**4.**　　　　　　　　　　] in the cold

14

weather. If this happens, they will also lose a lot of good things which are in the leaf, especially the nutrients they get from the soil.

❻ They use the nutrients to make chlorophyll and they don't want to lose them when the leaves freeze. So instead, they break down the chlorophyll to get the nutrients out and [⁵·   ] them in their roots, which are protected from the cold.

❼ As the plants break down the chlorophyll, the green color disappears from their leaves. What is left behind is other chemicals which you normally cannot see. The most important of these are called carotenoids, which are what makes carrots orange.

❽ Depending on which chemicals are found in the leaf, they can turn different [⁶·   ] of yellow or orange or even red. These chemicals do not have any nutrients in them, so the plant does not bother to break them down—it leaves them in the leaves.

❾ Once all the chlorophyll is taken out, the leaf dies. As it dries out, the leaf starts to look brown and becomes crispy. At this stage, it falls off the tree.

Notes
soil「土壌」 **chlorophyll**「クロロフィル［葉緑素］」 **food**「養分」 **photosynthesis**「光合成」
make a mess「散らかす」 **carotenoid**「カロテノイド」 **crispy**「パリパリした」

A 本文の内容に当てはまるものにはT、当てはまらないものにはFを（　　　）に書き入れましょう。

1. Plants need sunlight, water, and nutrients to grow. （　　　）

2. Summer is a better season for photosynthesis than winter. （　　　）

3. Cold weather is harmful for some plants because it destroys their leaves where nutrients are stored. （　　　）

B 葉の色が変わる仕組みについて表した以下の説明の（　　　）に適切な日本語を書き入れましょう。

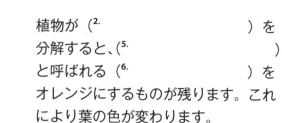

（¹.　　　　　　）をとらえるために、葉は（².　　　　　　　）と呼ばれる（³.　　　　　）を使います。それが葉を（⁴.　　）色にします。

植物が（².　　　　　　　　　）を分解すると、（⁵.　　　　　）と呼ばれる（⁶.　　　　　　）をオレンジにするものが残ります。これにより葉の色が変わります。

名詞を修飾する「分詞」を学習しましょう。

動詞の現在分詞形（-ing）や過去分詞形（-edなど）を使って、名詞を修飾することができます。
分詞の節が複数語になる場合は、名詞の前ではなく、後に置いて修飾するのが一般的です（後置修飾）。

例文 Chlorophyll turns sunlight into food, through a <u>process **called**</u> <u>photosynthesis</u>.
「クロロフィルは、<u>光合成と**呼ばれる**</u>過程を通して、日光を養分に変えます」

修飾される名詞が、その動詞の動作をおこなう〈主体〉となる場合 → 現在分詞
動作の〈対象〉である場合や、〈完了〉の意味合いを付加する場合 → 過去分詞

例）現在分詞　falling leaves「落ち葉（そのとき落ちているさなかの葉）」
　　過去分詞　fallen leaves「落ち葉（すでに落ちてしまった葉）」

Grammar for Practice

A （　　　）に適切な語を書き入れ、分詞を用いた文に書き換えましょう。

1. A man is speaking about the world's rarest plants. He is a famous botanist.
   → The man（　　　　　　　　　）about the world's rarest plants is a famous botanist.

2. She has received a letter from her student. It says that the color of the leaves has completely changed.
   → She has received a letter from her student（　　　　　　　）that the color of the leaves has completely changed.

3. The landowner cut down a tree. My grandfather deeply loved it.
   → My grandfather deeply loved the tree（　　　　　　　）down by the landowner.

B 日本語訳に合うように、[　　]内の語句を並べ替えましょう。

1. スクロースは楓の樹液から作られたシロップの中に見られる糖の一種です。

Sucrose is a type of sugar found _____

_____ .

[maple tree sap / the syrup / made / in / from]

2. 理科の授業の課題のために、枝の上でさえずっている小鳥を観察しなさい。

For the science class assignment, _____

on a branch.

[little / observe / the / birds / twittering]

One More Tip　順序・接続表現

聞いている人に分かりやすく説明するために、話の流れを明確にする表現を用いましょう。

■順序：First, ... / Next, ... / Finally, ...

　　　　First, ... / Second, ... / Third, ...

　　　　so / therefore / then / consequently

■逆接・対比：however / but / while / on the other hand / in contrast

■言い換え：in other words, ... / this is to say ... / for example, ...

■付加表現：in addition (to ...) / also / moreover / furthermore

Your Turn

本文を参照し、葉が落ちる過程を正しい順序になるように線で結びましょう。

First, the leaf ·　　　　　　　　　　　· falls off the tree.

Next, it　　·　　　　　　　　　　　· starts to dry out.

Finally, it　·　　　　　　　　　　　· looks brown.

また、上の表現を参考に、今日のあなたの行動を、ペアワークのパートナーに説明しましょう。

_____

_____

_____

Unit 3

Is It OK to Listen to Music While Studying?

Starting Words

1 〜 6 の語に合う英語と日本語の意味をそれぞれ選び、（　　）に書き入れましょう。

DL 019 　 CD1-19

Words	English Definitions	Japanese Definitions
1. conduct (　　)(　　)	**A** a person that you work with	**ア** 騒々しい
2. colleague (　　)(　　)	**B** to make something better than before	**イ** 環境
3. improve (　　)(　　)	**C** the conditions that are connected with and affect a situation	**ウ** 同僚
4. loud (　　)(　　)	**D** to do a particular activity	**エ** 求める
5. demand (　　)(　　)	**E** making a lot of noise	**オ** 改善する
6. circumstance (　　)(　　)	**F** to need a particular quality	**カ** おこなう

I Want to Know This!

枠内の問いについて、あなたならどのように答えますか。クラスで話し合いましょう。

I like to listen to music when I am studying, but some say it is better to leave my phone out of my room and concentrate on studying rather than listening to music. Is it OK to listen to music when I am studying?

_____

_____

_____

Here's a Key for You

次の英文は、前ページの問いに対する専門家による回答です。

A 音声を聴いて、[   ] に入る語を書き取りましょう。

B 英文を読んで理解しましょう。

🎧 DL 020 ～ 025　◉ CD1-20 ～ ◉ CD1-25

❶ In a nutshell, music puts us in a better mood, which makes us better at studying—but it also distracts us, which makes us worse at studying. You

5 may have heard of the Mozart effect — the idea that listening to Mozart makes you "smarter." This is based on research that found listening to complex classical music [¹·   ] test scores, which the researcher argued was based on the music's ability to stimulate parts of

10 our minds that play a role in mathematical ability.

❷ However, further research conclusively debunked this theory: it wasn't really anything to do with math, it was really just that music puts us in a better mood. Research [²·   ] in the 1990s found a "Blur Effect"—where kids who listened to the BritPop band Blur seemed to do better on tests. In fact,

15 researchers found that the Blur Effect was bigger than the Mozart effect, simply because kids enjoyed pop music more than classical music. Being in a better mood likely means that we try that little bit harder.

❸ On the other hand, music can be a distraction—under certain [³·   ] . When you study, you're using your "working

20 memory"—that means you are holding and manipulating several bits of information in your head at once. The research is fairly clear that when there's music in the background, and especially music with vocals, our working memory gets worse.

❹ Likely as a result, reading comprehension decreases when people listen to music with lyrics. Music also appears to be more distracting for people who are introverts than for people who are extroverts, perhaps because introverts are more easily overstimulated.

5 ❺ Some clever work by an Australia-based researcher called Bill Thompson and his [⁴.   ] aimed to figure out the relative effect of these two competing factors: mood and distraction. They had participants do a fairly [⁵.   ] comprehension task, and listen to classical music that was either slow or fast, and which was either soft or loud. They found the only time

10 there was any real decrease in performance was when people were listening to music that was both fast and [⁶.   ].

❻ But while that caused a decrease in performance, it wasn't actually that big a decrease. And other similar research

15 also failed to find large differences. To sum up: research suggests it's probably fine to listen to music while you're studying—with some caveats.

Notes

in a nutshell「一言でいうと」 **distract**「〜の気を散らす」 **Mozart**「モーツァルト（18世紀オーストリアの音楽家）」 **conclusively**「最終的に」 **debunk**「〜の誤りを指摘する」 **Blur**「ブラー（バンド名）」 **BritPop**「ブリットポップ（英国のポップ音楽）」 **manipulate**「〜を処理する」 **reading comprehension**「読解力」 **introvert**「内向的な人」 **extrovert**「外向的な人」 **overstimulate**「〜を過度に刺激する」 **relative effect**「相対効果」 **competing**「相反する」 **to sum up**「要するに」 **caveat**「注意事項」

A 本文の内容に当てはまるものには T、当てはまらないものには F を（　　　）に書き入れましょう。

1. Studying while listening to music is not recommended by the experts because of the Mozart effect. （　　　）

2. Classical music is more complex than pop songs, so you should study Mozart. （　　　）

3. According to research, there are no problems in listening to soft and slow instrumental music while studying. （　　　）

B 「ワーキングメモリ」について表した以下の説明の（　　　）に適切な日本語を書き入れましょう。

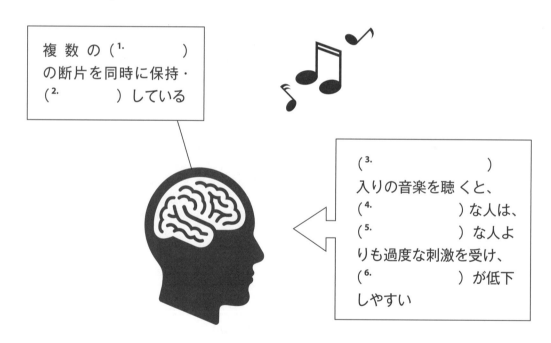

複数の（1.　　　　　）の断片を同時に保持・（2.　　　　　）している

（3.　　　　　　　　）入りの音楽を聴くと、（4.　　　　　　　）な人は、（5.　　　　　）な人よりも過度な刺激を受け、（6.　　　　　　　）が低下しやすい

For Better Understanding

「第5文型」（SVOC）の構造を学習しましょう。

英語の文の中には、〈主語（S）＋動詞（V）＋目的語（O：動作の対象となる語や節）＋補語（C：目的語の状態などを補足的に説明する語や節）〉という語順をとるものがあります。この並びを第5文型と呼びます。

例文 Music **makes** us better at studying.
　　　　 S 　　 V 　 O 　　　　 C
　　「音楽は私たちを、勉強するのによりよい状態に**します**」

第5文型をとる動詞は make、get、keep などが代表的です。

このとき、目的語と補語はイコールの関係で結ばれるのが特徴です。イコールで結ばれないものは第4文型（SVOO）と呼ばれています。

例）第5文型　 Music **makes** us happy.（us ＝ happy）
　　　　　　　　 S 　　 V 　O 　C
　　第4文型　 He **gives** us a book.（us ≠ a book）
　　　　　　　　 S 　 V 　 O 　 O

Grammar for Practice

A （　　　 ）に適切な語を書き入れ、第5文型に書き換えましょう。

1. Because of this excessively loud music, I feel sick.
   →　This excessively loud music makes me (　　　　　　　　　).

2. He was appointed as a conductor by the National Youth Orchestra.
   →　The National Youth Orchestra appointed (　　　　　　　) a conductor.

3. This guitar is called by its well-known nickname Rocky.
   →　People call this guitar (　　　　　　　). It's a well-known nickname.

B 日本語訳に合うように、[　　　]内の語句を並べ替えましょう。

1. 家の中で過ごさなければならない日々でも、サティのワルツはいつも私たちを幸せにしてくれます。

Even if we have to spend our days at home, _____

_____.

[Satie's waltz / makes / always / happy / us]

2. この絵の中のピアノの鍵盤の部分は、白いままにしておいてください。

Please leave the keys of _____ picture.

[in / this / white / the piano]

One More Tip　大きな数

理工系分野では、数表現の理解が必須です。大きな数を英語で読んだり、聴いて理解できるようにしましょう。

■ カンマとカンマの間の3桁の数を読み、その後単位表現を読みます。

【単位表現】trillion「1兆」 billion「10億」 million「100万」 thousand「千」

例 That music video has been played more than 3 billion times on YouTube.
「あのミュージックビデオはYouTubeで30億回以上再生されている」

例

1,234,567,890,123

one **trillion** , two hundred thirty-four **billion** , five hundred sixty-seven **million** , eight hundred ninety **thousand** , (and) one hundred twenty-three

---

Your Turn

大きな数を3つ書き、ペアで問題を出し合いましょう。自分が書いた数を英語で読み上げ、パートナーはそれを数字で書き取ります。答え合わせもしましょう。

1. あなたの数字 : (　　　　　　　) 　　パートナーの数字 : (　　　　　　　　)

2. あなたの数字 : (　　　　　　　) 　　パートナーの数字 : (　　　　　　　　)

3. あなたの数字 : (　　　　　　　) 　　パートナーの数字 : (　　　　　　　　)

Do Cats and Dogs Understand Humans?

Starting Words

1〜6の語に合う英語と日本語の意味をそれぞれ選び、(　　　)に書き入れましょう。

🎧 DL 026　◎ CD 1-26

Words	English Definitions	Japanese Definitions
1. evolve (　　) (　　)	**A**　reacting quickly	**ア**　区別する
2. represent (　　) (　　)	**B**　to understand how two or more things are different	**イ**　敏感な
3. associate (　　) (　　)	**C**　to understand the meaning of something	**ウ**　結びつける
4. sensitive (　　) (　　)	**D**　to gradually develop over a period of time	**エ**　解釈する
5. distinguish (　　) (　　)	**E**　to mean or show	**オ**　進化する
6. interpret (　　) (　　)	**F**　to connect things in one's mind	**カ**　表す

I Want to Know This!

枠内の問いについて、あなたならどのように答えますか。クラスで話し合いましょう。

I have a cat and two dogs. I want to communicate with them. Do cats and dogs understand humans when they make meowing or barking noises?

_____

_____

_____

Here's a Key for You

次の英文は、前ページの問いに対する専門家による回答です。
A 音声を聴いて、[   ] に入る語を書き取りましょう。
B 英文を読んで理解しましょう。

🎧 DL 027 ～ 034 ◎ CD1-27 ～ ◎ CD1-34

❶ There's been a lot of research about communication between people and domestic animals like dogs and cats. But we don't yet have the answer to your very interesting question. We don't know what cats and dogs think or if they understand us when we use their noises.

5 ❷ Our vocal chords are different from theirs, but they can hear that we make different sounds from what they do. And we know that dogs can definitely [¹·   ] between different people's voices. They'll know that it's Mila who's talking, and that it's Alex. They're also [²·   ] to your tone of voice. They like high-pitched, friendly tones.

10 ❸ And did you know that dogs can learn words? Rico, a border collie, successfully learned more than 200 words [³·   ] different items. He could pick the correct item from all the items if asked to "fetch" whichever item. We do not think that he actually learned the meaning of the words, but he was very good at [⁴·   ] different sounds with different objects.

15 ❹ When it comes to their own "voices," studies have shown that dogs and cats use different vocal signals to communicate different messages. A high-pitched, repetitive bark, for
20 example, may mean your dog is anxious. A low-pitched bark may mean  she's feeling aggressive. Cats also use certain sounds while hunting and others

26

when relaxing.

❺ But their "voices" are just one way in which dogs and cats communicate. They also use body language and tactile gestures, such as coming to you for a pat, or nudging your hand with their nose when they want attention.

5　❻ In the same way, people also communicate using gestures and facial expressions. Research has shown that dogs are better than other species, such as wolves, at [⁵.　　　　　　　　　　] our gestures and facial expressions.

❼ If you have dogs, you will notice that they're very sensitive to people's feelings and our ways

10 of communicating. That's because they've [⁶.　　　　　　　] to live in close proximity to people. Cats are not naturally social animals, but they also communicate with us and can be highly perceptive about what mood you're

15 in and how you're feeling.

❽ All of this is important when you think about the best ways to communicate with your dogs and cats. Since visual signals are really important to them, it's likely that they consider our body language, before listening to our sounds, so they can decide what it is that we're communicating.

Notes
  domestic animal「飼育動物」 **vocal chords**「声帯」 **border collie**「ボーダー・コリー（犬の一種）」 **fetch**「～を取ってくる」 **repetitive**「繰り返しの」 **aggressive**「攻撃的な」 **tactile gesture**「触れることによるジェスチャー」 **pat**「なでること」 **nudge**「～をつつく」 **close proximity**「とても近い状態」 **naturally**「本来は」 **perceptive**「気づいている」 **visual signal**「眼に見える信号」

What I Comprehended

A 本文の内容に当てはまるものには T、当てはまらないものには F を（　　　）に書き入れましょう。

1. Researchers have made it clear that dogs and cats can understand the exact meaning of what humans say to them. （　　　）

2. Both verbal and body languages are important to pets. （　　　）

3. Except for wolves, cats are the most sensitive to how people are feeling. （　　　）

B 本文で述べられている次の項目について、該当する動物の欄に分類しましょう。

① 誰が話しているのかを、その人の声で区別できる。
② 音と物体を結びつけることができる。
③ 獲物を追っている時とリラックスしている時では、鳴き声が異なる。
④ 人の顔の表情を理解する能力が、他の動物よりも高い。
⑤ 人に近い場所で暮らすように進化してきた。
⑥ 元来は社交的な動物ではない。

猫	犬

For Better Understanding

「名詞節を作る疑問詞」を学習しましょう。

疑問文に用いる what / who / where / why / how などの疑問詞は、動詞や前置詞に後続する名詞節を作ることができます。

　＊名詞節：主語と動詞のある文が名詞の働き（主語・補語・目的語になる）をするもの

・動詞の目的語になる

例文 1　　We don't know **what** cats and dogs think.

　　　　　　　　　　　　　　名詞節

　　　　　　「私たちは、猫や犬が**何を**考えているのか分かりません」

what ＋ 主語（cats and dogs）＋ 動詞（think）

→「猫や犬が何を考えているのか（ということ）」

・前置詞の目的語になる

例文 2　　Cats can be highly perceptive about **what mood** you're in.

　　　　　　　　　　　　　　　　　　　　　　　　　名詞節

　　　　　　「猫は、あなたが**どのような気分**なのかについて、よく気付くことができます」

what mood（どのような気分）＋ 主語（you）＋ 動詞（are）

→「あなたがどのような気分なのか（ということ）」

Grammar for Practice

A　日本語訳を参考に、（　　　）に入る疑問詞を選択肢から選びましょう。

1. We don't know for sure about (　　　　　　) cats and dogs understand humans.
私たちは、猫や犬がどのようにして人間のことを理解するのかについて、正確には知りません。

2. Dogs can tell (　　　　　　) voice they are hearing now.
犬は、今誰の声を聞いているのかを区別することができます。

3. A recent study showed (　　　　　　) dogs started to live with humans.
最近の研究で、犬が人間と一緒に住み始めたのはいつなのかが示されました。

where	when	how	whose

B 日本語訳に合うように、[   ] 内の語句を並べ替えましょう。

1. 身体言語は、ペットが私たちの異なる感情をどのように区別するのかについて研究する際の、もう一つの重要な要素です。

Body language is another key factor in _____

_____ between our different feelings.

[our pets / studying / distinguish / how]

2. 人間は、コミュニケーションの主要な方法として言語を用います。それが、私たちが自分の言葉に対してペットに反応してほしいと思う原因です。

Humans use language as our main means of communication. That's _____

_____ our words.

[we / respond to / want / to / why / our pets]

One More Tip　序数

順序を表す表現（序数）を学習しましょう。

one「1、1つの」→ first「1番目の、最初の」
two「2、2つの」→ second「2番目の」
three「3、3つの」→ third「3番目の」

fourth「4番目の」　fifth「5番目の」　sixth「6番目の」　seventh「7番目の」
eighth「8番目の」　ninth「9番目の」　tenth「10番目の」

twenty-first「21番目の」　thirty-second「32番目の」　forty-third「43番目の」

Your Turn

日本におけるパンダの歴史を調べて（　　　）に序数を書き入れ、ペアで確認し合いましょう。また、序数を使って身の回りのものを説明しましょう。

1. Lan Lan and Kang Kang were the (　　　　　　　) pandas that came to Japan from China in 1972.

2. Cai Bang was born in 2018 in Adventure World in Wakayama Prefecture. August 14, 2020 was her (　　　　　　) birthday.

3. _____

Unit 5

What Is Brain Freeze?

■ Starting Words

1 〜 6 の語に合う英語と日本語の意味をそれぞれ選び、（　　　　）に書き入れましょう。

 DL 035　CD1-35

Words	English Definitions	Japanese Definitions
1. typical (　　) (　　)	**A** full of activity, busy doing things	**ア** 刺激
2. nerve (　　) (　　)	**B** the part of your face between your eyes and hair	**イ** 典型的な
3. active (　　) (　　)	**C** having the usual features or qualities	**ウ** 額
4. stimulus (　　) (　　)	**D** to notice something	**エ** 神経
5. forehead (　　) (　　)	**E** inner body parts which connect the brain and other parts of the body	**オ** 感知する
6. detect (　　) (　　)	**F** something that makes something move or react	**カ** 活発な

■ I Want to Know This!

枠内の問いについて、あなたならどのように答えますか。クラスで話し合いましょう。

> When I ate an ice cream the other day, I suddenly got a terrible headache. My friend said it was "brain freeze." What is brain freeze? My friend doesn't know exactly what it is, either.

Here's a Key for You

次の英文は、前ページの問いに対する専門家による回答です。

A 音声を聴いて、[　　　] に入る語を書き取りましょう。

B 英文を読んで理解しましょう。

DL 036 ～ 043　　CD1-36　～　CD1-43

❶ Many of us probably have gobbled up an ice cream and perhaps too quickly. After doing this, you may have been unlucky enough to get an intense squeezing or stabbing sensation on your [**1.**　　　　　　　　　], your
5　temples, or the back of your head. This is brain freeze, also known as an "ice cream headache."

❷ Brain freeze is a bit weird. While it's true that you do put ice cream inside your head to eat it (your mouth is technically part of your head), you don't [**2.**　　　　　　　] put it into the parts
10　of your head that hurt when you experience brain freeze.

❸ So why do your forehead and temples (or even the back of your head) hurt when you put ice cream in your mouth too fast?

❹ When you cool down the roof of your mouth, the coldness is picked up by [**3.**　　　　　　　] cells that live there and whose job is to [**4.**　　　　　　　]
15　cold. This information about coldness is sent to your brain via a nerve. When the roof of your mouth is very cold, these cells (and so this nerve) will be very active.

❺ Now, these nerves also contain information from other cells, including the ones that detect cold and painful [**5.**　　　　　　　] from other parts of your head, including your face. It *may* be (we're honestly not sure) that when the cells that
20　sense cold in the roof of your mouth are very active, this *somehow* also activates the bits of the brain that are usually activated by the face cells. As a result, the cold fools

your brain into thinking that your forehead hurts.

❻ Another possibility is that as delicious icy treats quickly cool down our tongues and mouths, it actually cools the blood in blood vessels that supply blood to your head. These blood vessels respond by changing how much blood flows into your
5　brain. Only a few scientists have actually tried to measure this, and those that have don't even agree about whether there is more or less blood going into your head. Everyone, however, agrees that it hurts. It may be some combination of these two things: that [^{6.}   ] of nerves causes a change in how much blood is going into your head.

10　❼ To get the answer, scientists need to convince other people (politicians, other scientists, and members of the public) that they should be given the time and money to answer that question. Unfortunately, the availability of time and money are not as boundless as the curiosity of scientists.

❽ My advice? Stay curious. Eat ice
15　cream. Slowly.

Notes

gobble up ~「〜を素早く食べる」　**squeezing**「絞られるような」　**stabbing**「刺されるような」
sensation「感覚」　**temple**「こめかみ」　**weird**「へんてこな」　**roof of the mouth**「上あご」
via「〜を通して」　**the bits of the brain**「脳の細片」　**treat**「ごちそう」　**blood vessel**「血管」
availability「利用可能」　**boundless**「無限の」

What I Comprehended

A 本文の内容に当てはまるものには T、当てはまらないものには F を（　　）に書き入れましょう。

1. You have an ice cream headache when you put ice cream into the exact parts of your head where you feel pain. （　　）

2. There are nerves which detect cold in the roof of your mouth. （　　）

3. Both activation of nerves and the amount of blood which flows into your head can cause an ice cream headache. （　　）

B 「アイスクリーム頭痛」の原因を表した以下の図の（　　）に適切な日本語を書き入れましょう。

アイスクリームを口に入れると

――― 仮説① ―――
・ 上あごにある冷たさを感じる神経が頭部の冷たさや（1.　　　　　）の刺激を感知

・ 額が痛いのだと（2.　　　）が勘違い

――― 仮説② ―――
・ アイスクリームが舌と口を冷やす

・ 頭部へ流れる血管内の（3.　　　　　）を冷やす

神経の（4.　　　　　）

頭部への（5.　　　　　）の変化

アイスクリーム頭痛

For Better Understanding

「現在完了」の用法を学習しましょう。

過去との関連で現在の状態を表すときは、現在完了〈have ＋過去分詞〉を用います。
現在完了には〈経験〉〈継続〉〈完了・結果〉の３つの用法があります。
本文中では、以下のように〈経験〉の用法が用いられています。

例文 1　Many of us probably **have gobbled** up an ice cream. 〈経験〉
　　　　「多くの人たちは多分、アイスクリームを素早く食べたことがあるでしょう」
〈経験〉の用法ではしばしば、ever「これまでに～した」、never「～したことがない」、
before「以前」などが併せて用いられます。

例文 2　I **have been having** an ice cream headache for a minute. 〈継続〉
　　　　「私は１分間（ずっと）アイスクリーム頭痛がしています」
〈継続〉の用法では、〈for ＋期間〉や〈since ＋出来事の起点〉といった期間を表す語
句がしばしば用いられます。

例文 3　I **have** already **eaten** the ice cream. 〈完了・結果〉
　　　　「私はもうアイスクリームを食べてしまいました」
〈完了・結果〉の用法では、already「すでに～」、yet「まだ～」などが頻出です。

Grammar for Practice

A　日本語訳を参考に、（　　　）内の語を適切な形に書き換えましょう。

1. I (finish →　　　　　　　　　　　) reading the book on the nervous
system.
私は神経系に関するその本を読み終えてしまいました。

2. Have you (experience →　　　　　　　　　　　) an ice cream headache
before?
あなたはこれまでにアイスクリーム頭痛を経験したことがありますか。

3. The scientist (study →　　　　　　　　　　　　　) the relationship
between the amount of blood that flows into the brain and headaches for a
long time.
その研究者は脳に流れ込む血液量と頭痛の関係を長い間ずっと研究しています。

B 日本語訳に合うように、［　　　］内の語句を並べ替えましょう。

1. 多くの科学者が何十年も研究資金の不足に苦しんでいます。

Many scientists _____

of research funds for decades.

[suffering / the shortage / been / from / have]

2. 私はアイスクリームを大量にとても早く食べる時でさえ、アイスクリーム頭痛がしたことがありません。

I _____ even

when I eat a large amount of it very quickly.

[an ice cream headache / never / had / have]

<table>
<tr><td>One More Tip</td><td>分数・小数</td></tr>
</table>

分数・小数表現を英語で学びましょう。

■小数：小数点（point）以下の数は1桁ずつ数を読みます。

例 3.14 (three point one four)

■分数：分子を先に読み、次に分母を序数で読みます。分子の数が1より大きい場合は、分母は序数の複数形にします。複数形にし忘れることが多いので注意が必要です。「2分の1」、「4分の～」には特殊な読み方もあります。

例 $\frac{1}{3}$ (one[a] third)　$\frac{3}{5}$ (three fifth**s**)　$\frac{1}{2}$ (one[a] half)　$\frac{1}{4}$ (one[a] quarter / one[a] fourth)　$\frac{3}{4}$ (three quarter**s** / three fourth**s**)

例 A brain freeze started just after I had finished two fifths of all the ice cream.

「アイスクリーム全体のちょうど5分の2を食べ終わったところで、アイスクリーム頭痛が始まった」

Your Turn

小数・分数を3つ書き、ペアで問題を出し合いましょう。自分が書いた数を英語で読み上げ、パートナーはそれを数字で書き取ります。答え合わせもしましょう。

1. あなたの数字：(　　　　　　)　　パートナーの数字：(　　　　　　)
2. あなたの数字：(　　　　　　)　　パートナーの数字：(　　　　　　)
3. あなたの数字：(　　　　　　)　　パートナーの数字：(　　　　　　)

Unit 6

Why Does Reading in the Back Seat Make You Feel Sick?

DL 044　CD1-44

Starting Words

1 ～ 6 の語に合う英語と日本語の意味をそれぞれ選び、（　　）に書き入れましょう。

Words	English Definitions	Japanese Definitions
1. argument （　）（　）	**A** to solve a disagreement	ア　議論
2. cell （　）（　）	**B** not moving	イ　信号
3. settle （　）（　）	**C** a sound or action to deliver information	ウ　胃
4. signal （　）（　）	**D** the organ inside the body where food is digested	エ　細胞
5. still （　）（　）	**E** a discussion in which people have different views	オ　解決する
6. stomach （　）（　）	**F** the smallest part of an organism	カ　静止した

I Want to Know This!

枠内の問いについて、あなたならどのように答えますか。クラスで話し合いましょう。

> My father took us for a drive last weekend. My sister, who sat next to me, enjoyed it very much, but I got carsick because I was reading a book in the car. Why does reading in the back seat make me feel sick?

Here's a Key for You

次の英文は、前ページの問いに対する専門家による回答です。

A　音声を聴いて、[　　　] に入る語を書き取りましょう。

B　英文を読んで理解しましょう。

🎧 DL 045〜048　◎ CD1-45 〜 ◎ CD1-48

❶ The answer has to do with our eyes, our ears, and our brain. Reading in the back seat can make you feel sick because your eyes and ears are having an argument that your brain is trying to [¹.   ]! When you're reading in the back seat, your eyes see that your book is still. Your eyes then tell your brain you are still. But
5　your ears feel the car is moving. Your ears then tell your brain you're moving.

❷ Your ears don't just hear, they help with your balance too. Your ear has three main parts: the outer ear, the middle ear, and the inner ear. Your
10　inner ear contains [².   ] that have hairs sticking out the top. Scientists call these "hair cells." Some

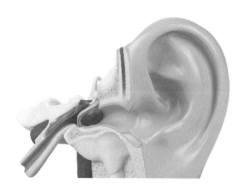

of these hair cells help us to hear. When sound hits those hair cells, the hairs move and the cells send signals to the brain. Our brains use those
15　[³.   ] to hear. Other hair cells help us to keep our balance. When the car we're sitting in moves, that movement makes the hairs on those hair cells move too, and they send different signals to the brain. Our brain uses those different signals to tell we're moving.

❸ Some people's brains don't like it when their eyes say they're [⁴.   ]
20　but their ears say they're moving. When eyes and ears argue like this, the brain can think that something dangerous might be about to happen. If this happens, the brain can get the body ready to fight or run away (scientists call this the "fight or flight" response). One of the things the brain can do is take blood away from the

[**5.**   ] to give to the muscles. Giving blood to the muscles can help us to fight or run away. But taking blood away from the stomach can make us feel sick.

❹ If reading in the back seat makes

5   you feel sick, you might need to settle the argument between your eyes and your ears. One way to do this is to stop reading and to look out the car window. But this suggestion won't

10   work for everyone. Some people will still feel sick when they ride in a car,

even if they aren't reading. This is because while our eyes and our ears help us to balance, so do our skin and our muscles. This creates many opportunities for [**6.**   ] that our brain has to settle!

Notes

have to do with ~「〜と関係がある」 **balance**「平衡感覚」 **outer ear**「外耳」 **middle ear**「中耳」 **inner ear**「内耳」 **stick out**「突き出る」 **hair cell**「有毛細胞」 **be about to do**「今にも〜する」 **get ~ ready**「〜に準備させる」 **fight or flight response**「闘争・逃走反応」

A 本文の内容に当てはまるものには T、当てはまらないものには F を（　　　）に書き入れましょう。

1. The inner ear helps us to balance by telling our brain that we are moving.
（　　　）

2. One signal from hair cells gives our brain the information that "we are hearing" and "we are moving." （　　　）

3. Everyone can recover from motion sickness when he or she stops reading and looks out the car window. （　　　）

B 車の後部座席で読書をしていて気分が悪くなる際、体の各器官には何が起こっているのか、以下の表の（　　　）に適切な日本語を書き入れましょう。

目	脳に（1.　　　　　　　　　　）と告げる	
耳	脳に（2.　　　　　　　　　　）と告げる	
脳	(3.　　　　　　　　　　　　　) が今にも起こるかもしれないと考え、体に、(4.　　　　　　) もしくは逃走する準備をさせる	
胃	血液が（5.　　　　　　　　　）	
筋肉	血液が（6.　　　　　　　　　）	

「動名詞」の用法を学習しましょう。

> 動詞を名詞として機能させたいとき、〈-ing〉に変化させることで、**動名詞**として用いることができます。
>
> | 例文 | **Giving** blood to the muscles can help us to fight or run away.
> 「血液を筋肉に**与えること**は、私たちが闘争したり逃走したりするのを助けることができます」
>
> 動名詞の規則
> ・「～すること」と訳す
> ・単数扱い（主語の場合）
> ・後ろに目的語などが続くことが多いが、これらが動名詞のまとまりとなる
>   give blood to the muscles「血液を筋肉に与える」
>   ↓
>   **giving** blood to the muscles「血液を筋肉に**与えること**」
>   このような動名詞のまとまりが、主語（～は）や目的語（～に、～を）や補語になります。

Grammar for Practice

A 日本語訳を参考に、以下の文が正しい文になるように１カ所、動名詞に書き換えましょう。

1. 異なる信号を脳に送ることは、私たちの気分が悪くなる原因になり得ます。
Send different signals to the brain can cause us to feel sick.

_____

2. お薦めの休日の過ごし方の一つは、ドライブに行くことです。
One recommended way to spend a holiday is go for a drive.

_____

3. 私は、耳の様々な機能について専門家と話すことを楽しみました。
I enjoyed talk with experts about many functions of our ears.

_____

B 日本語訳に合うように、[   ] 内の語句を並べ替えましょう。ただし、文頭の文字も小文字になっています。

1. 内耳の有毛細胞の重要性について議論することは、医学生にとって有意義です。

_____ in our inner ear

is significant for medical interns.

[of / hair cells / the importance / discussing]

2. もし車酔いをしたくなければ、後部座席でスマートフォンを操作するのを避けなければなりません。

If we don't want to get carsick, we _____

_____ in the back seat.

[a smartphone / avoid / must / using]

One More Tip 四則演算

数式の基本、四則演算を英語で学びましょう。

■四則計算：plus (+) / minus (−) / times[by] (×) / divide (÷)

例 $2 \times 4 = 8$ (Two times[by] four equals eight.)

$12 \div 6 = 2$ (Twelve divided by six equals two.)

Unit 3 と Unit 5 で学んだ「大きな数」や「小数・分数」を用いる場合も同様です。

例 $123,456.25 + 0.75 = 123,457$

(One hundred twenty-three thousand (and) four hundred fifty-six point two five plus zero point seven five equals one hundred twenty-three thousand (and) four hundred fifty-seven.)

$\frac{3}{4} - \frac{1}{2} = \frac{1}{4}$

(Three fourths[quarters] minus one[a] half equals one[a] fourth[quarter].)

距離・速さ・時間の法則：Speed is distance divided by time.

Your Turn

数式を3つ書き、ペアで問題を出し合いましょう。自分が書いた数式を英語で読み上げ、パートナーはそれを数字で書き取ります。答え合わせもしましょう。

1. あなたの数式 : (   )　　パートナーの数式 : (   )

2. あなたの数式 : (   )　　パートナーの数式 : (   )

3. あなたの数式 : (   )　　パートナーの数式 : (   )

Unit 7

Why Does Swiss Cheese Have Holes?

Starting Words

1 ～ 6 の語に合う英語と日本語の意味をそれぞれ選び、（　　　）に書き入れましょう。

DL 049　CD1-49

Words	English Definitions	Japanese Definitions
1. convert (　　)(　　)	**A** hard or firm in shape	ア　〜から発祥する
2. originate (　　)(　　)	**B** being like water	イ　変える
3. emit (　　)(　　)	**C** to change	ウ　栄養の
4. liquid (　　)(　　)	**D** to send out	エ　放出する
5. nutritional (　　)(　　)	**E** to appear for the first time	オ　固体の
6. solid (　　)(　　)	**F** relating to giving or gaining the food for being healthy	カ　液体の

I Want to Know This!

枠内の問いについて、あなたならどのように答えますか。クラスで話し合いましょう。

My mother likes cheese and bought many kinds of cheese yesterday. Each has a different shape and character. I want to know what makes them different. Especially, why does Swiss cheese have holes?

Here's a Key for You

次の英文は、前ページの問いに対する専門家による回答です。

A 音声を聴いて、[　　　]に入る語を書き取りましょう。

B 英文を読んで理解しましょう。

DL 050 ～ 056　CD1-50 ～ CD1-56

❶ There are thousands of kinds of cheese, each with its own color, shape, [1.　　　　　　　] value, flavor, and texture. Since cheese is made from milk, cheese types tend to vary based on the source of the milk. Some of the most popular cheeses are made from the milk of cows, goats, and sheep.

5 ❷ To make cheese, you need to add bacteria to the milk. These create chemical reactions that cause it to change into a combination of [2.　　　　　] "curds" and 10 [3.　　　　　] "whey." The whey

is generally drained off, concentrated, and dried into a powder. Variations in the amount and type of bacteria influence the taste and texture of the final product.

❸ Like many other cheeses, Swiss cheese is made with cow's milk and contains bacteria that help [4.　　　　　] the milk into a solid. So why does Swiss 15 cheese have holes? Also called "eyes," they're so essential to Swiss cheese that when they're missing, the cheesemakers say the batch is "blind."

❹ What makes Swiss cheese "holey" is additional bacteria called *Propionibacterium freudenrichii subspecies shermanii*—*P. shermanii* for short. Under the specific conditions that Swiss cheese is made, the *P. shermanii* produce a gas: carbon dioxide. 20 Because Swiss cheese is made at a warm temperature—around 70 degrees Fahrenheit—the cheese is soft and malleable. So as the bacteria grow, the gases they [5.　　　　　] end up creating round openings.

44

❺ Think of blowing a bubble with chewing gum: as you blow air from your lungs, the pressure forces the gum into a circle. The bubble eventually pops, due to air pressure from your lungs or the atmosphere.

But when a bubble has formed inside a hunk of warm cheese—and then that cheese is cooled to around 40°F—the hole stays in place. The cheese now has its eyes. It takes about four weeks at 70°F for the eyes to form. In total, it takes about six weeks to make Swiss cheese, and then it is aged two additional months before it is sold.

❻ Other countries are also known for cheeses that are similar to Swiss cheese. France has Gruyere, while Italy has Fontina. Gouda cheese—which [⁶·   ] in the Netherlands—is sometimes intentionally made with cultures that produce a little bit of gas and tiny eyes.

❼ But in most cases, cheesemakers actually try to prevent the formation of gas in their cheeses. Especially in harder cheeses, gas doesn't lead to nice, round eyes; instead, it forms unsightly crevices, cracks, and splits.

Notes

texture「食感」 curds「凝乳」 whey「乳清(乳漿)」 drain off ~「～を抜き取る」
concentrate「～を濃縮する」 cheesemaker「チーズ製造業者」 batch「一塊」 holey「穴あきの」 Propionibacterium freudenrichii subspecies shermanii「プロピオニバクテリウム・フロイデンライシイ亜種シャーマニイ」 Fahrenheit「華氏」 malleable「簡単に形が変わる、順応性がある」 opening「穴」 pop「破裂する」 hunk「大きな塊」 age「～を熟成させる」 Gruyere「グリュイエール(チーズ)」 Fontina「フォンティーナ(チーズ)」 Gouda cheese「ゴーダチーズ」 the Netherlands「オランダ」 culture「培養物」 unsightly「醜い」 crevice「裂け目」

A 本文の内容に当てはまるものには T、当てはまらないものには F を（　　）に書き入れましょう。

1. The taste and texture of cheese are influenced by the number of holes in the cheese. 　　　　　　　　　　　　　　　　　　　　　　　　　（　　　）

2. The reason Swiss cheese has holes is that bubbles are made inside warm cheese and then the cheese is cooled down. 　　　　　　　　　　（　　　）

3. It takes about 10 weeks for Swiss cheese to be made and arrive in stores. （　　　）

B スイスチーズに穴ができる仕組みについて、以下の表の答えの欄に適切な日本語を書き入れましょう。

質問	答え
P. シャーマニイと呼ばれる細菌が生み出す気体は？	1.
スイスチーズが作られるときの温度は？	2.
その温度により、チーズはどのような状態か？	3.
その状況下で、細菌が成長する際に放出される気体が作り出すものは？	4.

3つ以上の単語を並べる際の規則を学習しましょう。

等位接続詞の and や or を使うときに、3つ以上の単語を並べる際は、最後のみに and や or を用います。

例文 Some of the most popular cheeses are made from the milk of <u>cows, goats, and sheep</u>.
「もっともよく知られているチーズのうちのいくつかは、牛、山羊、羊の乳で作られています」

「牛」、「山羊」、「羊」の3つの単語が並んでいますが、cows と goats の間に and は用いられていません。このように、<u>3つ以上の単語を並列する際は、and や or は最後のみに用い、それ以外はコンマ（ , ）を用います</u>。よって、cows and goats and sheep や cows and goats, sheep とはなりません。

また、and や or の前にコンマが付かない場合もあります。以下のように覚えておきましょう。
A and B
A, B(,) and C
A, B, C(,) and D

Grammar for Practice

A 下線部を正しく書き換えましょう。

1. This cheese store has <u>Camembert and Cheddar and Gorgonzola</u> in stock.

→ This cheese store has _____ in stock.

2. These Japanese cheesemakers export their products to <u>China and Thailand and Indonesia and Cambodia</u>.

→ These Japanese cheesemakers export their products to _____

_____.

3. To make cheese, you need to add bacteria to the milk <u>and change it into curds and whey and drain off</u> the whey.

→ To make cheese, you need to add bacteria to the milk _____

_____ the whey.

B 日本語訳に合うように、[   ] 内の語句を並べ替えましょう。

1. 私が買って冷蔵庫に入れておいたチーズが、父か、母か、弟によって、食べられてしまいました。

The cheese I bought and stored in the refrigerator has been eaten by _____
_____.

[mother / my father / brother / , / , / or]

2. スイスチーズは、華氏約 70 度で作られ、華氏約 40 度まで冷やされ、2 カ月間熟成されます。

Swiss cheese is made at around 70°F, _____
_____ two months.

[aged / cooled / around 40° F / to / for / and / ,]

One More Tip 分類表現

雑多な情報も分類・整理し構造化することで、分かりやすくまとまった情報として相手に提示することができます。

例

Cheese	can be is	divided classified categorized sorted broken	into three	groups, types, kinds, categories,	such as ~. which include ~. A, B, and C.

Your Turn

身近にあるものを分類し、ペアワークのパートナーに説明しましょう。トピック・センテンス（P. 12 参照）から始めるように注意しましょう。

_____.

_____ is / are divided into _____

_____ , such as / which (is, are) _____

_____.

Unit 8

How Do Wounds Heal?

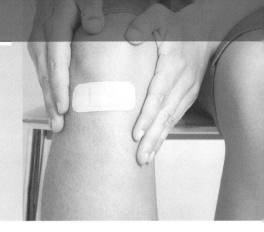

Starting Words

1 〜 6 の語に合う英語と日本語の意味をそれぞれ選び、（　　　）に書き入れましょう。

🎧 DL 057　◎ CD1-57

Words	English Definitions	Japanese Definitions
1. wound （　　）（　　）	**A**　to provide something	**ア**　体温
2. chemical （　　）（　　）	**B**　a mark on the skin after an injury has healed	**イ**　化学物質
3. temperature （　　）（　　）	**C**　the measurement of how hot somebody's body is	**ウ**　腫れる
4. swell （　　）（　　）	**D**　a substance obtained by a chemical process	**エ**　傷
5. supply （　　）（　　）	**E**　an injury to a part of the body	**オ**　供給する
6. scar （　　）（　　）	**F**　to become bigger	**カ**　傷跡

I Want to Know This!

枠内の問いについて、あなたならどのように答えますか。クラスで話し合いましょう。

Four days ago, I fell off my bike in an accident, and my knees got injured. They ached so badly then, but now the wounds are disappearing. I would like to know how wounds heal.

_____

_____

_____

Here's a Key for You

次の英文は、前ページの問いに対する専門家による回答です。

A 音声を聴いて、[ ] に入る語を書き取りましょう。

B 英文を読んで理解しましょう。

DL 058 ～ 064　CD1-58 ～ CD1-64

❶ To explain how the body heals a break in the skin, I first need to explain a bit about how skin works. It has three layers that protect us from germs and help our body keep the right [¹·　　　　　]. For

5　example, when our body gets too hot, we have sweat glands in the skin that release salty water to cool us down (it's like air conditioning in our bodies).

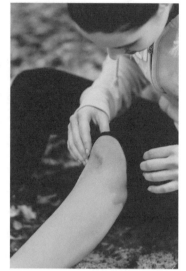

❷ Once we get a [²·　　　　], the first thing the body tries to do is stop the bleeding. Within minutes or

10　even seconds, tiny things in your blood called "blood cells" start to group together, protecting and plugging up the wound to stop any more bleeding. A scab will start to form.

❸ The body tries to plug up the wound as quick as it can. It wants to stop germs getting in through broken skin and making you really sick. But even as this happens,

15　the wound may let out a bit of clear fluid that helps to clean the wound.

❹ Under the skin, your body is hard at work cleaning and fixing. The wound may be [³·　　　　　], red, and painful. Doctors call this "inflammation." Swelling like this means the body is sending more fluid, oxygen, and blood cells to the wound to get to work fixing it.

20　**❺** In your blood there are special "soldier" cells in charge of fighting germs. They are called white blood cells, and as soon as you get a cut, your body will send a lot of

50

white blood cells to the wound to get to work.

❻ The blood cells in the body then work to start building new skin, layer by layer. One thing they do is tell the body to start producing more of a [⁴·   ] called "collagen" which helps the skin form new layers. It usually takes a few days for
5 a wound to heal fully, but it sometimes takes much longer. If you get a really big wound, you might get a [⁵·   ].

❼ It is important to keep the wound clean, damp, and covered to help it heal more quickly. Wounds that are left
10 uncovered are likely to dry out and are not protected from other injuries. Your skin is busy healing underneath. You should eat healthy food to help fuel your body while it fixes itself. Your body needs protein, carbohydrates, and vitamins.
15 These foods [⁶·   ] energy for healing your wound, and help your immune system fight germs.

Notes

   germ「ばい菌」 **sweat gland**「汗腺」 **blood cell**「血球」 **plug up ~**「～をふさぐ」 **scab**「かさぶた」 **inflammation**「炎症」 **in charge of ~**「～を担当して」 **white blood cell**「白血球」 **collagen**「コラーゲン」 **damp**「湿った」 **protein**「タンパク質」 **carbohydrate**「炭水化物」 **vitamin**「ビタミン」 **immune system**「免疫系」

A 本文の内容に当てはまるものには T、当てはまらないものには F を（　　）に書き入れましょう。

1. Human skin consists of several layers. （　　）

2. A wound becomes swollen when germs break down your immune system completely. （　　）

3. For quick recovery, it is very good to dry out a wound. （　　）

B 怪我をしたときの皮膚の働きについて表した以下のチャートの（　　）に適切な日本語を書き入れましょう。

(¹.　　　　) が集合する

⬇

傷を保護し、(².　　　　)

⬇

(³.　　　　) が (⁴.　　　　) とたたかう

⬇

(⁵.　　　　) という化学物質を生成し、
新たな (⁶.　　　　) をつくる

For Better Understanding

「不定詞」の用法を学習しましょう。

不定詞とは、主語や時制に合わせて変化しない形（原形）で使われる動詞をさす呼称です。
「to不定詞」は to と組み合わせ、名詞節・副詞節・形容詞節を作ります。

例文　**To explain** how the body heals a break in the skin,
　　　　　　　　　　副詞節
I first need **to explain** a bit about how skin works.
　　　　　　　　名詞節
「体がどのように皮膚の傷を治すのか**説明するために**、まずは皮膚がどのように働くのかについて少し**説明すること**が必要です」

want、need、hope など、これから起こること・したいことを表現する動詞は、しばしば〈to不定詞〉を目的語にとります。

形容詞節：alcohol **to disinfect** a wound「傷を**消毒するための**アルコール」

to を伴わない「原形不定詞」もあります。help は〈to不定詞〉と〈原形不定詞〉の両方の形をとることができます。
例）help our body **to keep** the right temperature「体が適温を保つのを助ける」
　　= help our body **keep** the right temperature（原形不定詞）

Grammar for Practice

A （　　　　）に適切な語を書き入れ、to 不定詞を用いた文に書き換えましょう。

1. You must wash your hands well before touching your scar.
   → Before touching your scar, (　　　　) (　　　　　　) (　　　　　　　)
   hands well is necessary.

2. If you eat well and sleep well, you can be out of the hospital as quickly as possible.
   → (　　　　) (　　　　) (　　　　　　) of the hospital as quickly as possible, eat well and sleep well.

3. The doctor said, "a healthy diet helps you recover from injuries."
   → The doctor said, "a healthy diet helps (　　　　　) (　　　　) (　　　　　)
   from injuries."

B 日本語訳に合うように、[   ] 内の語句を並べ替えましょう。ただし、文頭の文字も小文字になっています。

1. 子どもたちにとってさえ、この救急箱を使うのは簡単です。

It is easy even _____.

[this / kids / first aid kit / use / to / for]

2. 怪我をするのを避けるために、歩いているときはまっすぐ前を見なさい。

_____, look straight forward when you

are walking.

[to / injured / avoid / getting]

One More Tip 平面図形（flat figure）

たくさんある平面図形の中から、今回は基本的な図形について英語で学習しましょう。

square	rectangle	triangle	circle	ellipse
「正方形」	「長方形」	「三角形」	「円」	「楕円」

五角形	pentagon	六角形	hexagon	七角形	heptagon
八角形	octagon	九角形	nonagon	十角形	decagon

X角形：X-sided polygon

例 When you take a close look at your skin, you can see plenty of hexagons there.

「あなたの肌を近くで見れば、たくさんの六角形が見えるだろう」

Your Turn

以下のものの平面的な形を下線部に書き入れ、ペアワークのパートナーと確認し合いましょう。また、身の回りのものの形を説明しましょう。

1. A rice ball is _____.
2. A tire is _____.
3. A rugby ball is _____.
4. _____ is _____.

How Does a Curveball Curve?

Starting Words

1 ～ 6 の語に合う英語と日本語の意味をそれぞれ選び、（　　　　）に書き入れましょう。

DL 065　CD1-65

Words	English Definitions	Japanese Definitions
1. difference （　　）（　　）	A　a steady, continuous movement	ア　重力
2. gravity （　　）（　　）	B　in the direction that is in front of you	イ　渦巻き
3. flow （　　）（　　）	C　a circular movement of water, wind, smoke, etc.	ウ　流れ
4. forward （　　）（　　）	D　a way in which things are unalike	エ　放つ
5. whirlpool （　　）（　　）	E　to let something go free	オ　前方に
6. release （　　）（　　）	F　the force which attracts things to the center of the Earth	カ　差

I Want to Know This!

枠内の問いについて、あなたならどのように答えますか。クラスで話し合いましょう。

I am a pitcher of a baseball team. Our team is often knocked out of the competition. I want to win the next game, so I am trying to throw a curveball. How does a curveball curve?

_____

_____

_____

▬ Here's a Key for You

次の英文は、前ページの問いに対する専門家による回答です。

A 音声を聴いて、[   ] に入る語を書き取りましょう。

B 英文を読んで理解しましょう。

🎧 DL 066〜072　◎ CD1-66　〜　◎ CD1-72

❶ You may have seen a pitcher throw a curveball in baseball. It's a pitch that can confuse a batter because it looks like it's flying straight but then curves away as it crosses home plate.

❷ The pitcher puts a spin on the ball when they
5　[**1.**   ] it from their hand. This could be a "topspin" rotation, where the top of the ball spins forward while the ball hurtles towards the plate. That creates air pressure [**2.**   ] on the ball that cause
10　it to "break," or change direction.

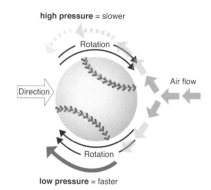

high pressure = slower

Rotation

Direction

Air flow

Rotation

low pressure = faster

❸ When the ball is spinning, it's dragging the air with it due to friction between the air and the ball. It's like there's a [**3.**   ] of motion of the air around the ball.

❹ As the ball is spinning, it slows down the air on the top of the ball. On the bottom,
15　the opposite is true. It's dragging the air with it as it rotates and moves towards the plate, speeding up the [**4.**   ] of air.

❺ So you've got this change in speed of the air between the top and the bottom of the ball. Lower speed air has higher pressure. Higher speed air has lower pressure.

❻ The difference in force acting on either side pushes the ball in a particular
20　direction. So if the ball is spinning [**5.**   ] with topspin, you have a

force pushing it down. If it's spinning to the side, there's going to be a force pushing it to the side.

❼ I study airplane aerodynamics, and there's a connection here—airplanes and baseballs have more in common than you might think. Airplane wings have low pressure on the top of the wing and higher pressure on the bottom of the wing. That pressure

difference creates a force that pushes the wing up, supporting the weight of the airplane against [⁶·   ] . It's the motion of air over the wing that creates those pressure differences that make an airplane fly. That pressure difference is the exact same principle that makes a baseball curve.

Notes
  pitch「投球」 **home plate**「本塁」 **spin**「回転」 **rotation**「回転」 **hurtle**「勢いよく飛んでいく」 **break**「カーブする」 **drag**「～を引っ張る」 **to the side**「横向きに」 **airplane aerodynamics**「航空力学」 **have in common**「共通点がある」 **principle**「原理」

A 本文の内容に当てはまるものには T、当てはまらないものには F を（　　　）に書き入れましょう。

1. If we throw a curveball with topspin, the ball curves upward when it reaches home plate. （　　）

2. If a ball is spinning to the left side, it is going to curve to the right side. （　　）

3. Airplane wings and curveballs with topspin rotate in the same direction. （　　）

B 野球のトップスピン回転と、航空機翼の仕組みについて、空気の圧力と速度が適切な組み合わせになるように線で結びましょう。

トップスピン回転

ボールの上部 ・　　　　・ 高圧力 ・　　　　・ 高速

ボールの下部 ・　　　　・ 低圧力 ・　　　　・ 低速

航空機翼

翼の上部 ・　　　　・ 高圧力 ・　　　　・ 高速

翼の下部 ・　　　　・ 低圧力 ・　　　　・ 低速

For Better Understanding

主格の「関係代名詞」を学習しましょう。

関係代名詞who / which / thatを使い、2つの文章を1つにまとめることができます。

That pressure difference creates a force. **It** pushes the wing up.

先行詞　　↓ 関係代名詞に変化

例文1 That pressure difference creates a force **that [which]** pushes the wing up.

「その圧力差が、翼を押し上げる力を生み出しています」

先行詞が人 → who / that　　先行詞が物や事物 → which / that

また、関係代名詞の前にコンマを置く形もあります。これを非制限用法と言い、先行詞に関する情報を付加する働きをします。

例文2 One of the techniques for playing tennis is a backspin rotation, **which** means the bottom of the ball spins forward.

「テニスをする際の技術の一つに、バックスピン回転があり、それはボールの下部が前方に回転することを意味しています」

Grammar for Practice

A (　　　) に適切な語を書き入れ、関係代名詞を用いた文に書き換えましょう。

1. The captain of my baseball team is Mike. He lives in the high-rise apartment building.

→　The captain of my baseball team is Mike (　　　　　) lives in the high-rise apartment building.

2. The ball is used for official games. It was made in Japan.

→　The ball (　　　　　) was made in Japan is used for official games.

3. The airplane developed by an American manufacturer has high-tech wings. They enable us to fly faster than ever.

→　The airplane developed by an American manufacturer has high-tech wings, (　　　　　) enable us to fly faster than ever.

B 日本語訳に合うように、[   ] 内の語句を並べ替えましょう。ただし、文頭の文字も小文字になっています。

1. 私たちに曲球の投げ方を教えられる監督が、技術の向上のために必要とされています。

_____ how to throw a curveball is

needed for the improvement of our skills.

[can / a coach / who / teach us]

2. 私は航空機がどのようにして飛ぶのかにずっと関心を持っているので、大学の専攻は、大気中の物体の動きを説明する空気力学です。

Since I've been interested in how the airplane flies, my academic major is

_____

of objects through the air.

[describes / aerodynamics / motion / , which]

One More Tip 立体図形 (solid figure)

立体図形の知識も重要です。たくさんの英語表現を学び、自分で説明できるようになりましょう。

sphere「球」　　cone「円錐」　　cube「立方体」　　cylinder「円柱」

「〜錐」: ~ pyramid　「〜柱」: ~ prism

三角錐	triangular pyramid	五角柱	pentagonal prism
四角錐	quadrangular pyramid	六角柱	hexagonal prism

例 A sphere is an object that is totally round, such as a baseball.
　　「球体とは、野球ボールのような完全に丸い物体のことである」

Your Turn

以下のものの立体的な形を下線部に書き入れ、ペアワークのパートナーと確認し合いましょう。また、身の回りのものの形を説明しましょう。

1. A dice is _____.

2. A planet is _____.

3. A fire extinguisher is _____.

4. _____ is _____.

Unit 10

Do Ants Have Blood?

Starting Words

1 ～ 6 の語に合う英語と日本語の意味をそれぞれ選び、（　　　）に書き入れましょう。

DL 073　CD1-73

Words		English Definitions	Japanese Definitions
1. lung （　　）（　　）	**A**	a substance that flows	**ア** 到達する
2. nutrient （　　）（　　）	**B**	to get to the place something has been travelling to	**イ** 肺
3. reach （　　）（　　）	**C**	a part of the body which performs a particular job	**ウ** 臓器
4. organ （　　）（　　）	**D**	to take air into the body and send it out again	**エ** 呼吸する
5. fluid （　　）（　　）	**E**	a substance which is needed for animals to live	**オ** 流動体
6. breathe （　　）（　　）	**F**	an organ in the chest with which animals breathe	**カ** 栄養

I Want to Know This!

枠内の問いについて、あなたならどのように答えますか。クラスで話し合いましょう。

The other day, I accidentally squashed some ants with my foot. But they didn't look like they were bleeding. Do ants have blood?

_____

_____

_____

Here's a Key for You

次の英文は、前ページの問いに対する専門家による回答です。

A 音声を聴いて、[   ] に入る語を書き取りましょう。

B 英文を読んで理解しましょう。

🎧 DL 074～82   💿 CD1-74 ～ 💿 CD1-82

❶ The short answer is ants have something similar to blood, but scientists call it "hemolymph." It is yellowish or greenish.

❷ In vertebrates (animals with backbones, such as humans, cats, dogs,
5 snakes, birds, and frogs) blood's main job is to move important things around the body. It moves stuff like [¹·   ] from our food, wastes, and oxygen from the air to

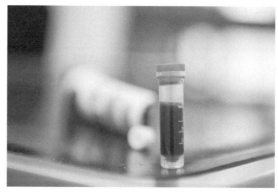

10 where it needs to go to make your body work properly. Your blood is red because it contains lots of tiny tiny packages called "red blood cells," which carry oxygen around your body.

❸ Ants and other insects also have a liquid inside their body that moves nutrients around. Although this [²·   ] does some of the same jobs as blood, it is
15 more correctly called hemolymph.

❹ An important difference between blood and hemolymph is that hemolymph does not move oxygen around the insect's body. The reason insect blood is usually yellowish or greenish (not red) is that insects do not have red blood cells. Unlike blood, hemolymph does not flow through blood vessels like veins, arteries
20 and capillaries. Instead it fills the insect's main body cavity and is pushed around by its heart.

❺ You might be wondering how insects move oxygen around their bodies without the help of red blood cells. The answer is that insects get oxygen to their [³.   ] in a very

5 different way than humans do.

❻ In humans, oxygen gets into our bodies through our mouth or nose and then goes to the lungs. The [⁴.   ] pass oxygen on to red blood cells, which carry oxygen around the body. Insects, on the other hand, [⁵.   ] through little holes on the side of their bodies called "spiracles." Each spiracle leads

10 to air tubes called trachea which branch through the entire body. The air tubes bring oxygen directly to the insect's organs without needing the help of red blood cells.

❼ The insect's breathing system doesn't work very well in larger animals because oxygen cannot travel far enough down the tubes to [⁶.   ] the organs. That's why insects are usually small.

15 ❽ About 250 million years ago when there was much more oxygen in the air, some insects did grow to amazing sizes. One type of dragonfly, for example, had wings that stretched almost a meter in length. That's about the distance an average adult covers in a single step!

❾ Blood and hemolymph are both amazing liquids that keep different types of

20 animals alive.

Notes

    hemolymph「体液」　**vertebrate**「脊椎動物」　**backbone**「背骨」　**red blood cell**「赤血球」
    blood vessel「血管」　**vein**「静脈」　**artery**「動脈」　**capillary**「毛細血管」　**body cavity**「体腔」
    spiracle「気門」　**trachea**「気管」　**branch**「枝分かれする」　**breathing system**「呼吸システム」　**dragonfly**「トンボ」

A 本文の内容に当てはまるものには T、当てはまらないものには F を（　　　）に書き入れましょう。

1. Ants also have red blood. （　　　）

2. Insects have a different breathing system from humans. （　　　）

3. In ancient times, some insects were bigger than now because the temperature was warmer. （　　　）

B 昆虫と脊椎動物の違いについて、以下の表の（　　　）に適切な日本語を書き入れましょう。

	昆虫	脊椎動物
栄養	(¹.　　　　　) が運ぶ — 黄や緑がかった色	(².　　　　　) が運ぶ — (³.　　　　　) が含まれるので赤い
酸素	(⁴.　　　　　) という穴から空気の管につながる	(⁵.　　　　　) が運ぶ — 鼻や口から取り入れられ、(⁶.　　) から赤血球へと受け渡される

For Better Understanding

「前置詞」の用法を学習しましょう。

前置詞には様々な種類がありますが、「前置詞の後ろには、名詞・動名詞（のまとまり）が来る」という共通のルールがあります。

例文1 Blood's main job is to move important things **around** the body.

 <u>名詞</u>

「血液の主要な仕事は大切なものを体中に運ぶことです」

* around「～のあちこちを」

例文2 The air tubes bring oxygen directly to the insect's organs

without <u>needing the help of red blood cells.</u>

 <u>動名詞</u>

「空気の管は、赤血球の助けを必要とせずに、昆虫の臓器に直接酸素を届けます」

* without「～なしに」

他にもたくさんの種類の前置詞があります。本文の中でも探してみましょう。

Grammar for Practice

A （　　　）に入る前置詞を選択肢から選びましょう。なお、複数回使うものもあります。

1. Red blood cells also remove carbon dioxide (　　　) your body, transporting it (　　　) the lungs for you to exhale.
赤血球はあなたの体から二酸化炭素を取り除き、吐き出すためにそれを肺にも運びます。

2. Insect immune systems are much different from a human's (　　　) terms of how they handle invaders.
侵入者にどのように対応するかという点で、昆虫の免疫システムは人間のものと非常に異なります。

3. Instead (　　　) having lungs and a heart or blood to deliver the oxygen, insects have a tracheal system that delivers the oxygen directly (　　　) each cell in the body.
酸素を運ぶために肺や心臓、血液を持つ代わりに、昆虫は体のそれぞれの細胞に直接酸素を届ける気管システムを持っています。

from	to	in	of	under	on

B 日本語訳に合うように、[   ] 内の語句を並べ替えましょう。

1. 何億年も前には、大気中の酸素量のため、巨大な昆虫は一般的でした。

Hundreds of millions of years ago, giant insects were common _____

_____ in the atmosphere.

[the amount / of / because / of / oxygen]

2. 科学者たちは、ツチボタルの数が全国で何十年も減少し続けていることを警告しています。

Scientists warn that the number of glowworms has been declining _____

_____ .

[the nation / decades / across / for]

One More Tip　図・位置関係

図を書くのに必要な表現を学びましょう。

■線・点 :point「点」　line「直線」　diagonal line「対角線」　curved line「曲線」
　　　　length「長さ」　intersection「交点」　horizontal「水平の」　vertical「垂
　　　　直の」

〔例〕　AB is a line 2 cm in length and parallel to line CD.
　　　「AB は 2 センチの直線で、線 CD に対し平行である」

■角度 :angle「角度」　degrees「〜度」　parallel「平行の」　perpendicular「直
　　　　角の」

〔例〕　The angle made by the lines EF and GH is 60 degrees.
　　　「線 EF と GH によって作られた角度は 60 度である」

〔例〕　This dragonfly is 20 cm in length and extends its wings
　　　perpendicular to its body.
　　　「このトンボは体長 20 センチで、体に対して直角に羽が生えている」

■その他 :diameter「直径」　radius「半径」

Your Turn

以下の図形について、**1.** 線 **AB** と線 **CD** の関係、**2.** 線 **AB** と線 **EF** の関係、**3.** 点 **G**
についてペアで説明し合いましょう。

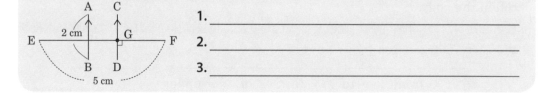

1.＿＿＿＿＿＿＿＿＿＿＿＿＿＿＿＿＿

2.＿＿＿＿＿＿＿＿＿＿＿＿＿＿＿＿＿

3.＿＿＿＿＿＿＿＿＿＿＿＿＿＿＿＿＿

Unit 11

How Does the Stuff in a Fire Extinguisher Stop a Fire?

Starting Words

1 〜 6 の語に合う英語と日本語の意味をそれぞれ選び、（　　　）に書き入れましょう。

DL 083　CD1-83

Words	English Definitions	Japanese Definitions
1. fuel （　　）（　　）	**A**　to move slowly in the air	**ア**　無臭の
2. oxygen （　　）（　　）	**B**　material used to produce heat or power	**イ**　浮く
3. float （　　）（　　）	**C**　without a smell	**ウ**　（息を）吐く
4. odorless （　　）（　　）	**D**　to breathe out air	**エ**　濃い
5. exhale （　　）（　　）	**E**　containing many people or things that are close together	**オ**　酸素
6. dense （　　）（　　）	**F**　a chemical element in air which is necessary for people	**カ**　燃料

I Want to Know This!

枠内の問いについて、あなたならどのように答えますか。クラスで話し合いましょう。

There are several fire extinguishers in my school. Why can we put out a fire with them? How does the stuff in a fire extinguisher stop a fire?

_____

_____

_____

次の英文は、前ページの問いに対する専門家による回答です。

A 音声を聴いて、[　　　] に入る語を書き取りましょう。

B 英文を読んで理解しましょう。

DL 084 ～ 090　CD1-84　～　CD1-90

❶ You need three ingredients to make fire: fuel (like wood or gasoline), oxygen, and heat. Fire is a chemical reaction between oxygen and the fuel. If you want to put out a fire, just get rid of one of those three things. Removing the fuel is easy. For example, when you shut off the gas valve on a propane grill, the fuel stops flowing
5 and the fire goes out.

❷ Removing the heat is harder to do. Once the fire starts, it provides heat and keeps burning. That is why throwing water on a fire puts it out.
10 When water hits fire it boils, turns to steam, and floats away, taking some heat with it. It also prevents [1.　　　] from reaching the fuel.

❸ Most fire extinguishers work by separating the fuel from the oxygen. The oxygen
15 comes from the air. Since the oxygen has to be in contact with the fuel, if you can coat the fuel with something that keeps the oxygen away, the fire will go out.

❹ Water isn't the only chemical that can put out fires. Carbon dioxide is an [2.　　　], colorless gas that is present in the air. People breathe in oxygen from the air and [3.　　　] carbon dioxide. That's exactly what happens when wood
20 burns. The fire uses oxygen and expels carbon dioxide. So carbon dioxide is sort of already burned — it won't burn if you throw it on a fire.

❺ Since carbon dioxide is a gas, it is easy to store and distribute. If squeezed into a steel canister, the gas streams out as you open the nozzle. Carbon dioxide is [**4.**　　　　　] than oxygen. So when you spray the carbon dioxide on fire, it sinks under the oxygen, separating the fire from oxygen. No oxygen, no fire.

5　❻ Carbon dioxide has several big advantages. Because the gas is squished into a canister, when it comes out it is super cold — at least minus 100 degrees Fahrenheit — removing heat from the fire. And when sprayed on a fire, carbon dioxide just [**5.**　　　　] away. When tossed on a fire, water will flow along the floor. This means water can spread the fire if the [**6.**　　　　] is light enough to be carried. So carbon
10　dioxide removes two out of the three things you need to have a fire. And, unlike water, carbon dioxide doesn't conduct electricity, so it is good for electrical fires.

❼ The biggest danger in using carbon dioxide is suffocation in enclosed spaces. In the same way that carbon dioxide puts out
15　a fire by robbing it of oxygen, the gas can do the same to a human.

Notes

get rid of ~「～を取り除く」 **gas valve**「ガス栓」 **propane grill**「プロパンガスのコンロ」
be in contact with ~「～と接触する」 **breathe in ~**「～を吸う」 **expel**「～を放出する」
sort of ~「いわば」 **distribute**「～を撒く」 **squeeze into ~**「～に押し込む」 **canister**「容器」
squish「～を押し込む」 **conduct**「(電気など)を通す」 **electrical fire**「漏電による火事」
suffocation「窒息」 **enclosed**「密閉された」 **rob A of B**「A から B を奪う」

■ What I Comprehended

A 本文の内容に当てはまるものには T、当てはまらないものには F を（　　）に書き
入れましょう。

1. Removing the heat is easier than removing the fuel because you can extinguish
a fire the moment you throw water on it.　　　　　　　　　　　　（　　）

2. Both humans and fire need oxygen and release carbon dioxide.　（　　）

3. One of the advantages carbon dioxide has is that it can be used for electrical
fires since it doesn't conduct electricity.　　　　　　　　　　　（　　）

B 二酸化炭素の消火器を用いた消火の仕組みについて表した以下のチャートの（　　）
に適切な日本語を書き入れましょう。

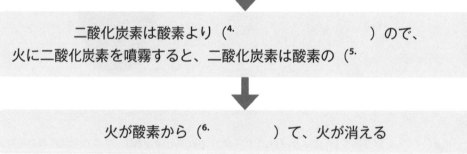

二酸化炭素を（1.　　　　　　　　　　　　　）に押し込める

（2.　　　　　　　　　　　）を開けると、
二酸化炭素が（3.　　　　　　　　）

二酸化炭素は酸素より（4.　　　　　　　　　）ので、
火に二酸化炭素を噴霧すると、二酸化炭素は酸素の（5.　　　　　　　）

火が酸素から（6.　　　　　）て、火が消える

For Better Understanding

現在分詞を用いた「分詞構文」を学習しましょう。

英語の書き言葉では分詞構文を用いて文を簡潔にすることがよくあります。

例文 When water hits fire it boils, turns to steam, and floats away, **taking** some heat with it.
「火に水がかかると水は沸騰し、蒸気になって浮動し、熱を連れていってしまいます」

分詞構文の作り方は、①接続詞（and / when / if など）と主語を省略し、②動詞を〈, + -ing 形〉に変形させます。

上の例文はもともと以下の文章から接続詞 and と主語 it を省略し、動詞 takes を〈, + taking〉に書き換えたものなのです。
When water hits fire it boils, turns to steam, and floats away, **and it takes** some heat with it.

Grammar for Practice

A （　　　）に適切な語を書き入れ、分詞構文を用いた文に書き換えましょう。

1. When you turn a gas stove on, the fuel starts flowing and reacts with oxygen and heat and makes a fire.
→ When you turn a gas stove on, the fuel starts flowing and reacts with oxygen and heat, (　　　　　　) a fire.

2. If you use carbon dioxide in an enclosed space, it fills the space and suffocates the people inside.
→ If you use carbon dioxide in an enclosed space, it fills the space, (　　　　　　　) the people inside.

3. The fire hit the forest, and it caused great destruction.
→ The fire hit the forest, (　　　　　　) great destruction.

B 日本語訳に合うように、[   ] 内の語句を並べ替えましょう。

1. 彼は突然立ち上がって、キャンプファイヤーのイベントを開催すべきではないと言いました。

He suddenly stood up, _____

 a campfire event.

[hold / we / that / should not / saying]

2. あなたが燃料を燃やすと、燃料は空気中の酸素と化学反応を起こし、熱を放出し、煙を生み出すのです。

When you burn fuel, it chemically reacts with oxygen from the air, _____

_____.

[smoke / heat / generating / and / releasing]

One More Tip　増減・構成表現

数や現象の増減や、実験対象の状態を説明する際に必要となる表現です。

■増減表現：rise, increase, climb「増加・上昇」
　　　　　　 fall, decrease, decline「減少・下降」
■変化の程度：sharply「急激に」　considerably「非常に」
　　　　　　 slightly「わずかに」　gradually「徐々に」
■構成：consist of ~, be composed of ~「～から成る」　contain「～を含む」
　　　　 be a compound of ~「～の化合物である」

　例　Salt (NaCl) is a compound of sodium and chlorine.
　　　「塩はナトリウムと塩素の化合物だ」

Your Turn

以下の化合物の構成を調べて下線部に書き入れ、ペアワークのパートナーと確認し合いましょう。別の化合物についても調べてみましょう。

1. H_2O is _____ two _____

　and _____.

2. HCl contains _____.

3. _____

Unit 12

Why Are Some People Affected by Sleep Paralysis?

Starting Words

1 〜 6 の語に合う英語と日本語の意味をそれぞれ選び、（　　　）に書き入れましょう。

🎧 DL 091　💿 CD1-91

Words		English Definitions	Japanese Definitions
1. pretty (　　) (　　)	A	a small problem or temporary delay	ア　とても
2. relax (　　) (　　)	B	not having the skill, strength, etc., to do something	イ　明滅する
3. hiccup (　　) (　　)	C	to keep going on and off	ウ　〜できない
4. chest (　　) (　　)	D	to become less tight or stiff	エ　胸
5. flicker (　　) (　　)	E	the top part of the front of the body .	オ　弛緩する
6. unable (　　) (　　)	F	very, quite	カ　小さな支障

I Want to Know This!

枠内の問いについて、あなたならどのように答えますか。クラスで話し合いましょう。

My friend told me that she sometimes suffers from a devil's curse. Actually, I can't believe it because her experience seems like the same thing as sleep paralysis. Why are some people affected by sleep paralysis?

_____

_____

_____

次の英文は、前ページの問いに対する専門家による回答です。

A 音声を聴いて、[　　　]に入る語を書き取りましょう。

B 英文を読んで理解しましょう。

🎧 DL 092 ~ 098　◎ CD1-92　~　◎ CD1-98

❶ Falling asleep is a bit like flicking off a light switch. One moment we are awake, but then the switch is flicked and we fall asleep. But sometimes, the switch gets a bit "sticky" and the light [¹·　　　　　　　] between being awake and asleep. This is what happens with sleep paralysis—when you wake up but feel like you can't

5　move.

❷ To answer your question, you're more likely to experience sleep paralysis if:

- someone in your family has it;
10 - you don't get enough sleep or you have changed your regular sleep pattern;

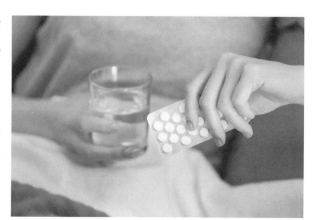

- you are a shift worker;

- you sleep on your back;

15 - you are stressed or taking certain medicines;

- you have a sleep disorder such as narcolepsy (which is where you fall asleep suddenly and uncontrollably when it's not really sleep time, like in class).

❸ Many people experience sleep paralysis at some stage, and it's usually first noticed in teenagers. It can affect men or women. Overall, though, there's still a lot

20　scientists don't know about sleep paralysis and why some people are more prone to it than others.

❹ In the olden days, some people called sleep paralysis the "Night Hag" and said it felt like a spooky witch or demon was sitting on your [²]. Now we know it is quite a common sleep problem, or what doctors call a parasomnia, caused by a little brain [³].

❺ With sleep paralysis, some parts of your brain are awake and still active but other parts are fast asleep. The sleeping part is the section of the brain that tells the muscles to [⁴] while we sleep so we don't act out our dreams. Evolution probably gave us that trick because acting out dreams can be harmful to yourself or others (although this trick doesn't always work and some people do act out their dreams).

❻ Sleep paralysis can feel [⁵] strange and scary, at least until you realize what is happening. If you are [⁶] to move or speak for a few seconds or minutes when falling asleep or waking up, then it is likely that you have what doctors call "isolated recurrent sleep paralysis."

❼ See your doctor if sleep paralysis continually prevents you from getting a good night's sleep. Your doctor may ask about how you're feeling, your health history, and if your family has had sleep problems. They may tell you to go to a specialist sleep doctor who can investigate further.

Notes
  flick off ~「(電灯)を消す」 **sticky**「厄介な」 **sleep paralysis**「金縛り」 **sleep on one's back**「仰向けで寝る」 **sleep disorder**「睡眠障害」 **narcolepsy**「ナルコレプシー（発作性睡眠）」 **prone to ~**「～する傾向がある」 **olden**「昔の」 **Night Hag**「夜の醜い老婆（「金縛り」の古い呼び方）」 **spooky**「不気味な」 **witch**「魔女」 **demon**「悪魔」 **parasomnia**「睡眠時随伴症」 **fast asleep**「熟睡して」 **feel**「～の感じを与える（自動詞）」 **isolated recurrent sleep paralysis**「反復性孤発性睡眠麻痺」

A 本文の内容に当てはまるものには T、当てはまらないものには F を（　　　）に書き入れましょう。

1. Sleep paralysis mainly occurs because of your actions in a dream.　（　　　）

2. Many people tend to experience sleep paralysis for the first time when they are under twenty.　（　　　）

3. Sleep paralysis happens when your body is awake but your brain is sleeping.　（　　　）

B 金縛りに遭う可能性が高い行動や性質について表した以下の図の（　　　）に適切な日本語を書き入れましょう。

(¹.　　　　　) にそういう傾向のある人がいる 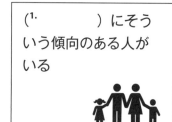	(².　　　　　) な睡眠がとれていなかったり、いつもの睡眠パターンが変わったりした	(³.　　　　　) である 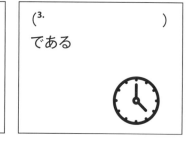
(⁴.　　　　　) で寝る 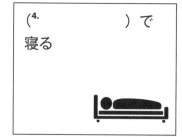	ストレスを感じたり、(⁵.　　　　　)を飲んでいたりする 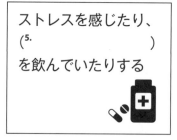	(⁶.　　　　　) がある 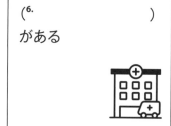

「無生物主語」を含む文を学習しましょう。

英語では、人や生き物ではなく、概念や事物（無生物）を主語にした文に出会うことがあります。

例文 1 **Evolution** probably gave us that trick because acting out dreams can be harmful to yourself or others.
「進化はおそらく、夢での動きを実際にしてしまうと自分自身や他人を傷つけてしまうかもしれないので、我々にこのようなごまかしを与えたのです」

make「～にする」、give「与える」、lead「導く」、leave「～にする」など以外にも、remind「思い出させる」、enable「～できるようにする」、allow「許可する」などの動詞との組み合わせで頻出し、原因・手段などを伝えます。

prevent は〈prevent ＋目的語となる人や物 ＋ from ＋ -ing〉の形で、「人・物が～するのを妨げる」という意味になります。

例文 2 **Sleep paralysis** continually prevents you from getting a good night's sleep.
「金縛りのせいで、良い睡眠をとることが継続的に妨げられます」

Grammar for Practice

A （　　　）に入る語を選択肢から選び、適切な形にして無生物主語を含む文に書き換えましょう。

1. I sometimes have a headache because of a bad dream.
   → A bad dream sometimes (　　　　　) me a headache.

2. A doctor invented a device. Thanks to that, people suffering from sleep with interrupted breathing can sleep well.
   → An invention made by a doctor (　　　　　) people suffering from sleep with interrupted breathing to sleep well.

3. Because he ate too many noodles, he could not go to bed until 2 a.m.
   → Eating too many noodles (　　　　　) him from going to bed until 2 a.m.

give	remind	enable	prevent

B 日本語訳に合うように、[   ] 内の語句を並べ替えましょう。

1. 適度な運動は、良い睡眠を与えます。

Moderate _____ .

[a / you / gives / good / exercise / sleep]

2. 「ジャーキング」という用語によって、うたた寝中の不快な経験について説明すること
ができます。

The term "jerking" _____

_____ while taking a nap.

[to / me / an / experience / explain / uncomfortable / allows]

One More Tip グラフ

データを示す際に活用されるグラフに関する英語表現について学習しましょう。

■グラフの種類：bar graph「棒グラフ」 line graph「折れ線グラフ」
　　　　　　　 pie graph「円グラフ」

例 The bar graph shows[indicates] that ....「棒グラフが示すように…」
　As you can see from the line graph, ...「折れ線グラフを見ると分かるように…」

■関連表現
　棒グラフ：The red bar is higher than ....「赤（い棒）は…よりも高い」
　線グラフ：horizontal axis「横軸」 vertical axis「縦軸」
　円グラフ：area / section / part「部分」 ratio / share / account for ~「占有率」

Your Turn

あなたの過去3日の睡眠時間を棒グラフに表し、ペアワークのパートナーに説明し
ましょう。

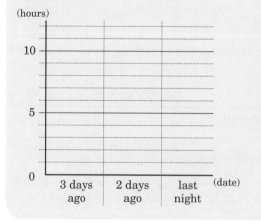

I slept _____ hours three
days ago, _____ hours two
days ago, and _____ hours
last night. As the bar graph indicates,
_____ .

Unit 13

How Do Ripples Form and Why Do They Spread Out Across the Water?

Starting Words

1 ～ 6 の語に合う英語と日本語の意味をそれぞれ選び、（　　　）に書き入れましょう。

 DL 099　　CD2-02

Words	English Definitions	Japanese Definitions
1. physics （　）（　）	**A** the top part of something	**ア** 原子
2. drag （　）（　）	**B** a group of atoms that forms a certain substance	**イ** 分子
3. shrink （　）（　）	**C** to pull something	**ウ** 物理
4. surface （　）（　）	**D** the smallest unit of a chemical element	**エ** 引く
5. atom （　）（　）	**E** the science that deals with light, heat, and other forms of energy	**オ** 表面
6. molecule （　）（　）	**F** to become smaller	**カ** 小さくなる

I Want to Know This!

枠内の問いについて、あなたならどのように答えますか。クラスで話し合いましょう。

When I was playing "splash rocks," I noticed that when I threw a rock into the river it made a circle shape, which got bigger. How does it make the ripple? Why do the circles spread out further and further? Why do they stop?

_____

_____

_____

Here's a Key for You

次の英文は、前ページの問いに対する専門家による回答です。

A 音声を聴いて、[   ] に入る語を書き取りましょう。

B 英文を読んで理解しましょう。

DL 100 〜 108　CD2-03 〜 CD2-11

❶ When you throw a rock into a river, it pushes water out of the way, making a ripple that moves away from where it landed. As the rock falls deeper into the river, the water near the [**1.**   ] rushes back to

5　fill in the space it left behind.

❷ The water usually rushes back too enthusiastically, causing a splash. The bigger the rock, the bigger the splash. The splash then creates even more ripples that tend to move away from where the rock went into the water.

10　❸ When water is in its calmest, lowest energy state, it has a flat surface. By throwing the rock into the river, you have given the water some energy. That causes the water to move around, trying to spread out the energy so it can go back to having a still, flat surface.

❹ This follows a powerful principle of [**2.**   ] , which is that

15　everything seeks to find a state where its energy is as small as possible.

❺ One way energy can move around is by forming waves. For example, the waves you see at the beach are formed by energy from the wind. Light and sound also move in waves,

20　though we can't see that directly. And the ripples that you see in the river are small waves

carrying away the energy from where you threw the rock.

❻ You might already know that everything you can touch is made up of lots of tiny molecules, which are themselves made up of even smaller parts called [³·   ].

5   ❼ Water is also made of [⁴·   ]. But during a ripple, the water molecules don't move away from the rock, as you might expect. They actually move up and down. When they move up, they [⁵·   ] the other molecules next to them up. Then they move down, dragging the molecules next to them down too.

❽ That's what creates the peaks and troughs you see on the surface of the water.
10 And that's how the ripple travels away from your rock—a bit like a human wave around a stadium.

❾ Dragging neighboring water molecules up and down is hard work, and slowly uses up energy, so the ripples get smaller as they get further away. Eventually, the ripples use up all the energy from the rock and the splash, and [⁶·   ]
15 until we can no longer see them.

Notes

ripple「波紋」 **enthusiastically**「激しく」 **splash**「水しぶき」 **low energy state**「低エネルギー状態」 **spread out ~**「～を拡散させる」 **still**「穏やかな」 **principle**「法則」 **trough**「谷」 **neighboring**「近くにある」 **eventually**「最終的に」

A 本文の内容に当てはまるものには T、当てはまらないものには F を（　　　）に書き入れましょう。

1. The larger the rock you throw into a river, the larger the splash it causes.

（　　）

2. Ripples in a river are waves which contain a sort of energy.　（　　）

3. The ripples become smaller as the amount of energy in them increases.　（　　）

B 波紋が生まれるプロセスをまとめた以下の説明の（　　　）に適切な日本語を書き入れましょう。

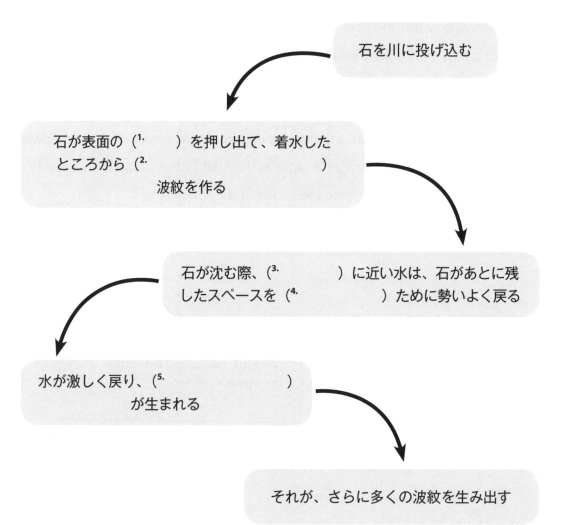

石を川に投げ込む

石が表面の（1.　　　）を押し出て、着水したところから（2.　　　　　　　　　）波紋を作る

石が沈む際、（3.　　　　）に近い水は、石があとに残したスペースを（4.　　　　　　）ために勢いよく戻る

水が激しく戻り、（5.　　　　　　　　）が生まれる

それが、さらに多くの波紋を生み出す

For Better Understanding

〈動詞＋ X ＋ to do〉の構文を学習しましょう。

動詞の中には、〈動詞＋ X ＋ to 不定詞〉という構文で使用するものがあります。X は先行する動詞の目的語であると同時に、後続する to 不定詞の意味上の主語でもあります。

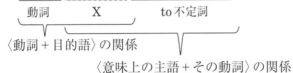

この構文で使用可能な動詞には、次のようなものがあります。
expect「期待する」、allow「許可する」、request「要求する」、cause「〜させる」、advise「助言する」、enable「〜できるようにする」、encourage「激励する」、ask「求める」、tell「命令する」、force「強いる」、want「〜してほしい」etc.

Grammar for Practice

A 日本語訳を参考に、（　　　）に入る語を選択肢から選び、必要があれば適切な形に書き換えましょう。

1. My little sister (　　　　　　) me to throw a stone into the river to make a splash.
川に石を投げて水しぶきをたてるよう、妹が私に求めました。

2. I picked up a big stone to throw, which (　　　　　) me to make a bigger splash.
私は大きな石を拾い上げて投げたところ、より大きな水しぶきをたてることができました。

3. The strong wind (　　　　　) waves to surge high and rock a ship on the sea.
強風によって波が高くうねり、海にある船を揺らしました。

| enable | ask | cause |

B 日本語訳に合うように、［　　　］内の語句を並べ替えましょう。

1. 沈んでいく石が、近くにある水の分子も川の中深くに沈みこませました。

The sinking rock _____

_____ into the river.

［ the neighboring water molecules / to / forced / deeper / also sink ］

2. スタジアムでのビッグウェーブが選手たちを激励し、試合で実力を発揮させました。

The big wave in the stadium _____

_____ the game.

［ to / in / the players / encouraged / show their talents ］

One More Tip 物理関連

「波紋」のような身近な現象にも、様々な物理法則を見ることができます。

■〜の法則：Hooke's law「フックの法則」 law of conservation of mass「質量
　　　　　保存の法則」 law of entropy「エントロピーの法則」 Ohm's law
　　　　　「オームの法則」 Newton's equation of motion「ニュートンの運動
　　　　　方程式、$F = ma$（F: Force, m: mass, a: acceleration）」
■〜定数：spring constant「ばね定数」 elastic constant[coefficient]「弾性定数」
■〜効果：tunneling effect「トンネル効果」 Doppler effect「ドップラー効果」
■〜力：buoyant force「浮力」 (dynamic) lift[lifting] force「揚力」
　　　　resistance force「抵抗力」 electromagnetic force「電磁力」
　　　　(internal) stress「応力」 pressure「圧力」
　　　　gravitation / attractive force「引力」
■〜エネルギー：heat[thermal] energy「熱エネルギー」 mechanical energy「機
　　　　　　　械エネルギー」 chemical energy「化学エネルギー」

Your Turn

ニュートンの運動方程式について説明した以下の英文の下線部に適切な語を書き入
れましょう。さらに他の項目を１つ選んでペアで発表し合いましょう。

Newton's equation of motion is $F = ma$, which means _____
is equal to _____ times _____.

Is the Sky Blue on Other Planets?

Starting Words

1 ～ 6 の語に合う英語と日本語の意味をそれぞれ選び、（　　　）に書き入れましょう。

DL 109　　CD2-12

Words	English Definitions	Japanese Definitions
1. expose (　　)(　　)	**A** very small in size or amount	**ア** 反応する
2. thick (　　)(　　)	**B** to have something inside or include something as a part	**イ** さらす
3. react (　　)(　　)	**C** to show something that is usually hidden	**ウ** 厚い
4. contain (　　)(　　)	**D** to move up or away after hitting a surface	**エ** 跳ね返す
5. tiny (　　)(　　)	**E** having a large distance between opposite sides	**オ** 含む
6. bounce (　　)(　　)	**F** to change in a chemical way when put with another substance	**カ** とても小さい

I Want to Know This!

枠内の問いについて、あなたならどのように答えますか。クラスで話し合いましょう。

My favorite color is blue, especially a clear sky on a June morning. Is the sky blue on other planets like on Earth? What is an atmosphere, and do other planets have one?

_____

_____

_____

Here's a Key for You

次の英文は、前ページの問いに対する専門家による回答です。

A 音声を聴いて、[　　　]に入る語を書き取りましょう。

B 英文を読んで理解しましょう。

🎧 DL 110～115 ⦿ CD2-13 ～ ⦿ CD2-18

❶ Atmospheres can [¹·　　　　　]
a wide variety of gases. Most of Earth's
atmosphere is a gas called nitrogen
that doesn't really [²·　　　　　]

5　with anything. There's also a fair bit of
oxygen, which is what we need to
breathe. There are also two other
important gases called argon and carbon dioxide, and [³·　　　　　] amounts of
lots of other ones. The mix of gases is what gives a planet's atmosphere its color.

10　❷ Earth's atmosphere is made up of gases that tend to [⁴·　　　　　　　] blue
light in all directions (known as "scattering") but let most other colors of light
straight through. This scattered light is what gives Earth's atmosphere its blue color.

❸ Do other planets have blue atmospheres? The atmospheres of the two ice giants
in our solar system, Neptune and Uranus, are both beautiful shades of blue.
15　However, these atmospheres are a different blue than ours. It's caused by the huge
amounts of a gas called methane swirling around. Uranus' atmosphere also contains
some ammonia, which makes the planet a slightly greener shade than the deep blue
we see on Neptune. However, there are some planets that have no atmosphere at
all! The Sun's closest and smallest neighbor, Mercury, is one example. Its surface is
20　[⁵·　　　　　　　　] to the vastness of space.

❹ So far I've been talking about the atmospheres of planets in our solar system. But
what about planets in other planetary systems, orbiting other stars? Astronomers

have been detecting the atmospheres of these planets (which we call "exoplanets") for the past 20 years! It wasn't until last year, however, that astronomers managed to
5 detect the atmosphere of a rocky exoplanet.

❺ The planet is called LHS 3844b and it's so far away that its light takes almost 50 years to reach us! LHS 3844b weighs twice as much as Earth, and we astronomers thought it would have a pretty [⁶.   ] atmosphere. But, to our surprise, it has little to no atmosphere at
10 all! So it might be more like Mercury than Earth.

❻ We still have a lot to learn about far-off planets, and discovering one with an Earth-like atmosphere that's ripe for life is still many years away. Maybe you could be the first astronomer to detect an Earth-like atmosphere on another world!

Notes

nitrogen「窒素」 argon「アルゴン」 be made up of ~「～で構成されている」 scattering「散乱」 scattered「散乱した」 giant「巨星」 solar system「太陽系」 Neptune「海王星」 Uranus「天王星」 methane「メタン」 swirl around ~「～を取り巻く」 ammonia「アンモニア」 Mercury「水星」 vastness「広大さ」 planetary system「惑星系」 orbit「～の軌道をまわる」 astronomer「天文学者」 exoplanet「太陽系外惑星」 It wasn't until ~ that ...「～になってようやく…した」 manage to do「なんとか～する」 far-off「はるか遠く離れた」 ripe「絶好の」

A 本文の内容に当てはまるものには T、当てはまらないものには F を（　　　）に書き入れましょう。

1. Earth's atmosphere contains not only nitrogen and oxygen, but also carbon dioxide. 　　　　　　　　　　　　　　　　　　　　　　（　　　）

2. Earth is the only planet in our solar system whose color is blue. 　（　　　）

3. Today, astronomers know enough about the atmosphere of any exoplanet but they cannot find any planet like Earth. 　　　　　　　　（　　　）

B 地球が青い仕組みについて表した以下の説明の（　　　）に適切な日本語を書き入れましょう。

地球の大気には（¹·　　　　　）、かなり多くの（²·　　　　　）、アルゴンと（³·　　　　　）、その他の気体が含まれる

これらの気体は、（⁴·　　　）光をあらゆる方向に（⁵·　　　　　）けれども、その他の光は（⁶·　　　　）通す

▬ For Better Understanding

仮説・可能性を表す「助動詞」を学習しましょう。

仮説や可能性が低いことを述べるときは、過去のことを話す場合以外でも、過去形の助動詞を使って表現することができます。例えばcouldは「〜できた」という〈可能〉の意味以外にも、「〜できうる」という〈可能性〉を述べる文章で頻出します。willの過去形would「〜だろう」も同様に、現在の状況の表現に利用できます。

*その他の仮説・可能性を表す助動詞：
  should「〜すべきである」、might「〜かもしれない」

例文 1 It **might** be more like Mercury than Earth.
「地球というよりは水星のほうにより似ている**かもしれません**」

例文 2 Maybe you **could** be the first astronomer to detect an Earth-like atmosphere on another world!
「もしかしたらあなたは、別世界で地球のような大気を検出する最初の天文学者になることが**できるかもしれません**よ！」

▬ Grammar for Practice

Ⓐ 助動詞を含む以下の文の日本語訳を完成させましょう。

1. Once I could say all the names of the astronauts in JAXA, because I really dreamed of working with them.
私はかつて、宇宙航空研究開発機構（JAXA）の宇宙飛行士の名前を全員分、
（　　　　　　　　　　　　　　　　　　　）。本当にその人たちと働くことを夢見ていたからです。

2. I like blue skies. I might look at them endlessly if I had no school.
私は青空が好きです。もし学校がなかったら、永遠に空を（
　　　　　　　　　　　　　）。

3. He gave me wrong information about tomorrow's astronomy exam. An honest man would not tell a lie.
彼は明日の天文学の試験について、私に間違った情報を伝えました。正直な人間ならば嘘を（　　　　　　　　　　　　　　　　　　）。

B 日本語訳に合うように、[   ] 内の語句を並べ替えましょう。ただし、文頭の文字も小文字になっています。

1. もし僕が宇宙の秘密を発見すれば，その発見は僕たちの生活を変えるだろう。

If I found the secret to space, _____

_____.

[the / our / discovery / transform / would / lives]

2. もし有名な惑星が消滅したら、彼女はショックをうけるかもしれません。

If a certain famous planet disappeared, _____.

[be / might / shocked / she]

One More Tip 数の接頭辞

数に関連する接頭辞を覚えておくと便利です。日常で見かけるものもありますね。centimeter、deciliter など、単位の構成要素になっているものもあります。

倍数		乗数		マイナス乗数	
mono-	1つの	deca-	10	deci-	10^{-1}
di-	2つの	hecto-	10^2	centi-	10^{-2}
tri-	3つの	mega-	10^6	milli-	10^{-3}
tetra-	4つの	giga-	10^9	micro-	10^{-6}
penta-	5つの	tera-	10^{12}	nano-	10^{-9}

Your Turn

これらの数に関連する接頭辞のついた語で知っているものを3つ書き出しましょう。また、なぜその接頭辞がついているのかをペアで話し合いましょう。

1. (   )

2. (   )

3. (   )

Unit 15

How Did I Get My Own Unique Set of Fingerprints?

⏻ DL 116　◉ CD2-19

Starting Words

1 ～ 6 の語に合う英語と日本語の意味をそれぞれ選び、（　　）に書き入れましょう。

Words	English Definitions	Japanese Definitions
1. blood vessel (　　)(　　)	**A**　to put information into another form	**ア**　変化しない
2. friction (　　)(　　)	**B**　the force that makes it difficult for an object to slide	**イ**　遺伝子
3. fingerprint (　　)(　　)	**C**　a small tube through which blood flows in your body	**ウ**　指紋
4. gene (　　)(　　)	**D**　firmly fixed or not likely to change	**エ**　血管
5. stable (　　)(　　)	**E**　a part of the DNA in a cell	**オ**　コード化する
6. encode (　　)(　　)	**F**　the pattern of curved lines on the end of a finger	**カ**　摩擦

I Want to Know This!

枠内の問いについて、あなたならどのように答えますか。クラスで話し合いましょう。

> I have found that everyone, from babies to old people, has fingerprints on their fingertips, and they vary from person to person when I look at them closely. How do we get the fingerprints we have?

_____

_____

_____

次の英文は、前ページの問いに対する専門家による回答です。

A 音声を聴いて、[   ] に入る語を書き取りましょう。

B 英文を読んで理解しましょう。

🎧 DL 117 〜 124 ◎ CD2-20 〜 ◎ CD2-27

❶ Fingerprints are those little ridges on the tips of your fingers. They're essentially folds of the outer layer of skin, the epidermis.

❷ Your [**1.**   ] began to form before you were born. When a fetus starts to grow, the outside layer of its skin is smooth. But after about 10 weeks,

5　a deeper layer of skin, called the basal layer, starts growing faster than the layers above it, which makes it "buckle" and fold. The expanding lower layer ends up scrunched and bunched beneath the outside layer.

❸ These folds eventually cause the surface layers of the skin to fold too, and by the time a fetus is 17 weeks old—about halfway through a pregnancy—its fingerprints

10　are set. Although this folding process might sound random, the overall size and shape of fingerprints are influenced by the [**2.**   ] you get from your parents. So you probably share some fingerprint patterns with your family members.

❹ But the details of your fingerprints are influenced by many other factors

15　besides genes. For example, the shape and size of the [**3.**   ] vessels in your skin, how fast the different layers of skin are growing, and the chemical environment inside the

20　womb all play a part. No two people end up with exactly the same fingerprints, even identical twins.

❺ It was only in 2015 that a big long-term study showed that fingerprints are [⁴·   ] over a person's lifetime. The ridges of a fingerprint are visible on the skin's surface layer, but the pattern is actually "[⁵·   ]" below that. Even if you have a major skin injury, your prints will come back when the outer

5   layer heals—though you might have a scar, too. So your fingerprints are totally unique to you and have been since before you were born. No matter how much you change as you grow up, you'll always have the set you have now, no matter how long you live.

❻ Surprisingly, nobody really knows what

10   fingerprints are for. People have long thought that fingerprints provide the [⁶·   ] that helps our hands grip objects. This makes sense because the other animals besides human beings that

15   have fingerprints—including many other

primates like apes and monkeys, and koalas—are all tree climbers.

❼ But sometimes what makes sense isn't true, and a recent study found that fingerprints don't really help people hold on to things—at least, not things with smooth surfaces.

20   ❽ Other possibilities are that fingerprints improve your sense of touch or help protect your fingers from injury. But scientists don't know for sure yet.

Notes

ridge「(一般に細長い) 隆起部」 fold「ひだ」 epidermis「表皮」 fetus「胎児」 basal layer「基底層」 buckle「ねじれる」 scrunched「くしゃくしゃになる」 bunched「まとまる」 pregnancy「妊娠期間」 womb「子宮」 identical twins「一卵性双生児」 It was only ~ that ...「…したのはようやく~だ」 make sense「理にかなう」 primate「霊長類」 ape「類人猿」

A 本文の内容に当てはまるものには T、当てはまらないものには F を（　　　）に書き入れましょう。

1. Fingerprints are formed in the middle of pregnancy. 　　　（　　　）

2. Identical twins sometimes have exactly the same fingerprint. 　　（　　　）

3. Recent research showed that our fingerprints are set to produce the friction which helps us grip objects. 　　　（　　　）

B 指紋についてまとめた以下の表の（　　　）に適切な日本語を書き入れましょう。

指紋	形状	・小さな（1.　　　　　　　　） ・表皮の（2.　　　　　）
	形成	妊娠約（3.　　　　　　）週後に基底層と呼ばれる皮膚の（4.　　　　　　）部分の層がそれより上にある層より早く形成し始め、そのことで（4.　　　　　）部分の層に「ねじれ」やひだを生じさせ，最終的に皮膚の表面の層のひだも生じさせる。
	特徴	・両親からの（5.　　　　　　　　　）に影響を受ける ・一生を通じて変化しない
	役割	明らかになっていない

94

For Better Understanding

「受動態」の用法を学習しましょう。

主語が動作主である「能動態」に対し、「受動態」は主語が動作・行為（動詞）の受け手になる場合に用います。受動態は、〈be動詞＋過去分詞（＋ by 動作主）〉で表します。

例文 1　The details of your fingerprints **are influenced by** many other factors besides genes.
「指紋の細かい部分は、遺伝子の他に多くの他の要素から影響を受けています」

また、能動態と受動態は書き換え可能な場合もあります。

例文 1'　Many other factors besides genes influence the details of your fingerprints.（能動態）

例文 2　These folds eventually **cause** the surface layers of the skin to fold.（能動態）
→ The surface layers of the skin **are** eventually **caused** to fold **by** these folds.（受動態）
「これらのひだが最終的に、皮膚の表面の層のひだを生じさせます」

Grammar for Practice

A　日本語訳を参考に、（　　　　）内の動詞を必要があれば適切な形に書き換えましょう。

1. Fingerprint data (scan → 　　　　　　　　　　　　) by the smartphone.
　指紋データはスマートフォンによってスキャンされました。

2. The image clearly (show → 　　　　　　　　　　) the blood vessel.
　この画像は血管を鮮明に描写したものです。

3. Most animals which (have → 　　　　　　　　　　) fingerprints
　(consider → 　　　　　　　　　　　　) to climb trees.
　指紋を持つ多くの動物は、木に登ると考えられています。

B 日本語訳に合うように、[　　　]内の語句を並べ替えましょう。

1. 指紋データは、指紋入力装置を使った機械によって取得されます。

Fingerprint data _____

_____ a fingerprint input device.

[the machine / which / acquired / by / uses / is]

2. いわゆる「静脈パターン」を検出するために、多くの研究が行われているところです。

A lot of research _____ so-called

"venous patterns."

[done / being / detect / is / to]

One More Tip　因果関係

「原因」と「結果」をつなげる表現を学びましょう。主語が動作主か動作の受け手かによって、動詞を能動態・受動態で使い分ける必要があります。

原因 （主語）	→ （能動態）	結果
The basal layers	cause	the ridges on your fingertips.
Genes	influence	the size and shape of fingerprints.
A skin injury	does not lead to	any change in your fingerprints.

結果 （主語）	→ （受動態）	原因
The ridges on your fingertips	are caused	by the basal layers.
The size and shape of fingerprints	are influenced	by genes.
Any change in your fingerprints	is not led	by a skin injury.

Your Turn

上記の表現を参考に、AI 技術が原因で生じた結果を説明しましょう。また、これまでテキストで学んできた以下の話題の中から一つ選択して復習し、原因と結果を明確にしながらペアで説明し合いましょう。

1. AI technology causes _____ .
2. _____

fingerprints	chlorophyll	ice cream headache	curved ball

Acknowledgements

All the materials are from The Conversation and reprinted by permission of the authors of the materials.

Text Credits

Unit 1 Why Is Air Colder the Higher Up You Go?

Curious Kids: why is air colder the higher up you go?

Authors: Zoran Ristovski (Queensland University of Technology), Branka Miljevic (Queensland University of Technology)

https://theconversation.com/curious-kids-why-is-air-colder-the-higher-up-you-go-116822

Unit 2 Why Do Leaves Change Color?

Curious Kids: why do leaves change colour?

Author: Giles Johnson (University of Manchester)

https://theconversation.com/curious-kids-why-do-leaves-change-colour-105318

Unit 3 Is It OK to Listen to Music While Studying?

Curious Kids: is it OK to listen to music while studying?

Author: Timothy Byron (University of Wollongong)

https://theconversation.com/curious-kids-is-it-ok-to-listen-to-music-while-studying-125222

Unit 4 Do Cats and Dogs Understand Humans?

Curious Kids: do cats and dogs understand us when we miaow or bark?

Author: Quixi Sonntag (University of Pretoria)

https://theconversation.com/curious-kids-do-cats-and-dogs-understand-us-when-we-miaow-or-bark-107383

Unit 5 What Is Brain Freeze?

Curious Kids: what is brain freeze?

Author: David Farmer (University of Melbourne)

https://theconversation.com/curious-kids-what-is-brain-freeze-112774

Unit 6 Why Does Reading in the Back Seat Make You Feel Sick?

Curious Kids: why does reading in the back seat make you feel sick?

Author: Wayne Wilson (The University of Queensland)

https://theconversation.com/curious-kids-why-does-reading-in-the-back-seat-make-you-feel-sick-128693

Unit 7 Why Does Swiss Cheese Have Holes?

Why does Swiss cheese have holes?

Author: Stephanie Clark (Iowa State University)

https://theconversation.com/why-does-swiss-cheese-have-holes-130451

Unit 8 How Do Wounds Heal?

Curious Kids: how do wounds heal?

Authors: Christina Parker (Queensland University of Technology), Helen Edwards
      (Queensland University of Technology), Kathleen Finlayson (Queensland
      University of Technology)

https://theconversation.com/curious-kids-how-do-wounds-heal-118603

Unit 9 How Does a Curveball Curve?

Curious Kids: How does a curveball curve?

Author: Jim Gregory (The Ohio State University)

https://theconversation.com/curious-kids-how-does-a-curveball-curve-108568

Unit 10 Do Ants Have Blood?

Curious Kids: do ants have blood?

Author: Tanya Latty (University of Sydney)

https://theconversation.com/curious-kids-do-ants-have-blood-108925

Unit 11 How Does the Stuff in a Fire Extinguisher Stop a Fire?

Curious Kids: How does the stuff in a fire extinguisher stop a fire?

Author: Joseph Lanzafame (Rochester Institute of Technology)

https://theconversation.com/curious-kids-how-does-the-stuff-in-a-fire-extinguisher-stop-a-fire-120859

Unit 12 Why Are Some People Affected by Sleep Paralysis?

Curious Kids: why are some people affected by sleep paralysis?

Author: Danny Eckert (Flinders University)

https://theconversation.com/curious-kids-why-are-some-people-affected-by-sleep-paralysis-121125

Unit 13 How Do Ripples Form and Why Do They Spread Out Across the Water?

Curious Kids: how do ripples form and why do they spread out across the water?

Author: Simon Cox (Aberystwyth University)

https://theconversation.com/curious-kids-how-do-ripples-form-and-why-do-they-spread-out-across-the-water-120308

Unit 14 Is the Sky Blue on Other Planets?

Curious Kids: is the sky blue on other planets?

Author: Jake Clark (University of Southern Queensland)

https://theconversation.com/curious-kids-is-the-sky-blue-on-other-planets-129779

Unit 15 How Did I Get My Own Unique Set of Fingerprints?

How did I get my own unique set of fingerprints?

Author: Sarah Leupen (University of Maryland, Baltimore County)

https://theconversation.com/how-did-i-get-my-own-unique-set-of-fingerprints-128391

本書にはCD（別売）があります

In Science Curiosity

好奇心から始める科学

2021年 1 月20日　初版第 1 刷発行
2024年 2 月20日　初版第 5 刷発行

編著者　　大塚　生子

瀧川　宏樹

清川　祥恵

監修者　　椋平　淳

発行者　　福 岡 正 人

発行所　　株式会社　金 星 堂

（〒101-0051）　東京都千代田区神田神保町 3-21
Tel　（03）3263-3828（営業部）
（03）3263-3997（編集部）
Fax　（03）3263-0716
http://www.kinsei-do.co.jp

編集担当　池田恭子　　　　　　　　Printed in Japan
印刷所・製本所／株式会社カシヨ
本書の無断複製・複写は著作権法上での例外を除き禁じられています。
本書を代行業者等の第三者に依頼してスキャンやデジタル化することは、
たとえ個人や家庭内での利用であっても認められておりません。
落丁・乱丁本はお取り替えいたします。

ISBN978-4-7647-4123-2　C1082